"Full of golden nuggets! It will appeal to those curious about art therapy to seasoned professionals/supervisors, and everyone in between. This graphic guide provides an answer to the age-old question, 'Art therapy, what is that?'"

—*Carolyn Brown Treadon, PhD, ATR-BC, ATCS, professor and Graduate Program Director at Edinboro University*

"Huxtable, Wolf Bordonaro and Schmanke provide a comprehensive pictorial digest and welcome contribution to the literature on the art therapy profession. The wonderful illustrations of culturally diverse art therapy practitioners and populations depict the breadth of information necessary to understand the scope of art therapy practice. I predict this graphic compendium will become a valuable resource for the nascent and seasoned art therapist."

—*Cheryl Doby-Copeland, PhD, ATR-BC, LPC, LMFT, Clinical Program Coordinator, Parent Infant Early Childhood Enhancement Program, and Honorary Life Member of the American Art Therapy Association*

"The authors hit upon the perfect formula: applying pictorial language to communicate to those who rely on visual communication to provide service for others. Their wonderfully engaging introduction to art therapy provides an accessible and fun foundation for those who simply want to learn more about art therapy, those who are committed to pursuing this calling, and those well embedded in the field."

—*David E. Gussak, PhD, ATR-BC, Professor of Art Therapy at Florida State University and Project Coordinator of the FSU/FDC Art Therapy in Prisons Program*

T0301182

A GRAPHIC GUIDE TO

Art Therapy

AMY E. HUXTABLE

with GAELYNN P. WOLF BORDONARO
and LIBBY SCHMANKE

Jessica Kingsley Publishers
London and Philadelphia

First published in Great Britain in 2022 by Jessica Kingsley Publishers
An Hachette Company

1

The list on p.123 is reproduced from Rappaport, L. (2016) "Focusing-Oriented Art Therapy." In J.A. Rubin (ed.) *Approaches to Art Therapy: Theory and Technique* (3rd ed.). New York, NY: Routledge, p.288. Reproduced with permission of the Licensor through PLSclear.

Front cover image source: Amy E. Huxtable

A CIP catalogue record for this title is available from the
British Library and the Library of Congress

ISBN 978 1 78775 351 8
eISBN 978 1 78775 352 5

Printed and bound in the United States by Integrated Books International

Jessica Kingsley Publishers' policy is to use papers that are natural, renewable and recyclable products and made from wood grown in sustainable forests. The logging and manufacturing processes are expected to conform to the environmental regulations of the country of origin.

Jessica Kingsley Publishers
Carmelite House
50 Victoria Embankment
London EC4Y 0DZ

www.jkp.com

Table of Contents

Acknowledgments

I've always enjoyed writing, but I never really saw any of my work as worthy of publishing until Libby Schmanke and Gaelynn Wolf Bordonaro entered my life. Libby and Gaelynn have supported this book from beginning to end. They helped me find resources, provided crucial feedback on the content and graphics, and guided me through the publication process. Suffice it to say that this book would not have been possible without their expertise, and I am so grateful to have such generous, knowledgable, and encouraging mentors.

I would like to thank Morgan Ford Willingham, who provided valuable critiques on the illustrations, layout, font, alignment, and spacing to make this book as esthetically appealing as possible. In a graphic novel, the illustrations are just as important as the words, so I was grateful to receive Morgan's feedback.

Of course, I must also acknowledge the art therapists, psychologists, and mental health professionals who have already written about the topics and vignettes covered in this book. While constructing this graphic novel, I had the pleasure of learning from originators of theories, developers of assessments, researchers who have published articles on special populations, and textbook authors who have summarized the field of art therapy. I am certainly indebted to these writers.

Thank you to Jessica Kingsley Publishers for accepting my proposal and providing an opportunity to have my work published. In particular, I would like to acknowledge Elen Griffiths and Simeon Hance for their help in developing this book.

I would also like to thank the following folks for their emotional support.

To my colleagues at Emporia State University, who are now wonderful mental health professionals: Kaitlyn Ekart-Eliot, Vivian Mosier, Wendy Lynch, Samantha "Larry" Lawrence, Anna Brink, and Claire Becker. As much as a student can learn from their professors, I certainly learned just as much from all of you. Thank you for inspiring me throughout our studies and beyond!

To the expressive therapy team at The University of Kansas Health System, Marillac Campus: Janet Glenski-Peterson, Jane Twyman, Ross Stone, and Becca Kurtz. Once a week, without fail, at least one of you would ask, "How's your book coming along?" Somehow, you were still willing to listen to my woes after a whole year and a half of asking! Thank you also for showing me firsthand what it means to be an expressive therapist. Your delightful sense of humor has really kept me going.

To the folks at the School Leadership/Middle and Secondary Teacher Education department at Emporia State University: Trish Irwin, Amanda Lickteig, and Dan Stiffler. Thank you for your support during the beginning stages of this book!

To my spouse, Grahm Mahanna, who is my biggest cheerleader. When I was hesitant about my ability to write and illustrate an entire book, you helped me view the task through a more positive lens. When I was stressed about the smallest of details, you helped me take a step back and look at the big picture. Thank you for always believing in me and supporting my creative endeavors.

To my mom, dad, brother, sister-in-law, and nephews. Thank you for checking in on the progress of this book and offering much-needed words of encouragement and motivation.

Oh, and thanks to my cats.

Preface

Back in November 2018, I was an anxious mess of a graduate student trying to figure out some options for my capstone project. I knew I wanted to make use of my background in graphic design, but that was as far as I could get on my own.

I met with my professors Libby Schmanke and Gaelynn Wolf Bordonaro for guidance, and after some brainstorming, they recommended that I write an educational graphic novel about art therapy. Without need for further consideration, I hopped on board. I mean, I had the opportunity to illustrate characters and write goofy dialog to help people learn. What could be better?

After looking up resources about graphic novels in education, I better understood the value of an illustrated textbook about the field. I will spare you my entire literature review and instead provide you with my conclusion.

> *Art therapists complete a rigorous graduate program in order to practice ethically. Art therapy coursework spans a variety of topics and concepts, some of which may be difficult to learn through text alone. Graphic novels provide an engaging and effective way for students to learn material through a concise, informative, and even humorous format. Based on this evidence, a supplementary graphic textbook could be a helpful tool to meet the educational needs of art therapists-in-training.*

Although I had originally planned for this book to be beneficial for undergraduate and graduate students (and so I still hope it will be), I also reflected on my own discovery of art therapy. I had worked as a graphic designer for two years and had already begun to feel uninspired and jaded. I didn't want to stray away from a creative field, but I knew that what I was doing wasn't sustainable. I did too much searching online before finding any information about art therapy.

While talking to my colleagues at Emporia State University, I learned that my story wasn't unique. Most of my peers stated that they didn't *really* know what art therapy was before they entered our master's program. What I often heard was something similar to "I like art, and I want to help people...so here I am."

I suppose what I'm getting at is that although art therapy is a growing field, the profession doesn't seem to be on many people's radar. I am hopeful that this succinct, illustrated book is both appealing and non-threatening for people who have an interest in learning more about the field.

And, of course, a part of me hopes that this book finds its way into the hands of a young person who is unaware of art therapy but likes art and wants to help people.

Introduction

So...hello there!
How are you?

My guess is that you've picked up this book to gain a better understanding of art therapy.

Perhaps you're a graduate student studying art therapy now! Good for you!

Or maybe...

You have an interest in studying art therapy in the future?

Your friend is an art therapist, and you can't quite grasp what they do, but you want to be a supportive friend?

You just like books with pictures in them? Who doesn't?

Regardless of what enticed you to pick up this book...welcome!

Let's start out with a general overview of art therapy before we get into the really fun stuff.

What Is Art Therapy?

Art therapy is a mental health profession in which a trained art therapist works with clients to meet individualized goals. Art making is used as a means of self-expression, containment, and communication.

Art therapists work with clients of all ages and meet with...[1]

Individuals

Groups

Couples and Families

Communities

What Are Some Goals of Art Therapy?

Art therapists and clients develop a therapeutic relationship in which they work to identify and reach personal or relational goals.

Here are a few common goals.[2]

Reducing symptoms associated with depression, anxiety, trauma, and grief

Improving cognitive and motor function

Enhancing social skills

What Are Some Goals of Art Therapy?

These are only a few of the many goals art therapy can support. Later on, we will add more specific goals to the list when we discuss art therapists' work with special populations.

Common Misconceptions

Art therapy is a growing field that is often misunderstood.[3] Art therapists and art therapists-in-training might hear a few of these statements and questions; part of getting involved in the field means accurately describing and advocating for the profession.

Art Therapy, Therapeutic Art, and Art Classes

Let's go back to those folks on the "common misconceptions" page. They seem to be a little confused about how art therapy differs from therapeutic art and art classes. Although the three often overlap, it is important to understand how they are different.

Let's see if this diagram[4] can clear up some of the confusion.

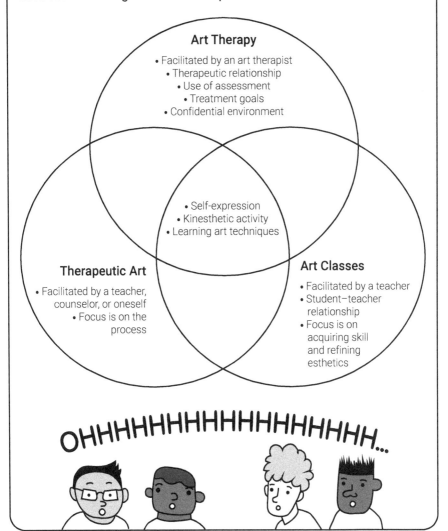

Art Therapy
- Facilitated by an art therapist
- Therapeutic relationship
- Use of assessment
- Treatment goals
- Confidential environment

- Self-expression
- Kinesthetic activity
- Learning art techniques

Therapeutic Art
- Facilitated by a teacher, counselor, or oneself
- Focus is on the process

Art Classes
- Facilitated by a teacher
- Student–teacher relationship
- Focus is on acquiring skill and refining esthetics

OHHHHHHHHHHHHHHHHH...

Why Art Therapy?

Rubin outlined several reasons why visual art is beneficial in the therapeutic process.[5]

Why Art Therapy?

Triangular Relationship

Art therapy is different from other therapies, because it requires a three-way process.[6] Let's see how that works.

The relationship between the art therapist and the client is the most important.

Art Therapist

Client

Art Product

Qualifications

Art therapists are trained as both therapists and artists; they must earn a master's degree before practicing.[7] Let's see which of these candidates is qualified to practice art therapy.

> I've been teaching art for 20 years!

Nope!

Having the experience of teaching art is great! However, a master's in art therapy is required before this person can practice.

> I'm a licensed social worker, and I sometimes include art in my sessions.

Getting closer...but no.

Mental health professionals can implement art into their sessions, but this does not make them art therapists!

> I took an online art therapy class one time!

Not yet...

Some online sources boast that they can teach art therapy through short-term courses. This might be a good start in exploring the field, but it does not make someone qualified to practice art therapy.

> I earned my master's degree in art therapy, and I am registered to practice!

Ding, ding, ding!

We have a winner!

Education

What are some of the educational requirements for art therapists?

> I majored in art, but I took enough psychology credits to qualify for a master's program.

> I earned bachelor's degrees in both psychology and studio art.

Prerequisite Undergraduate Education

In the United States, students typically earn their bachelor's degrees in art or psychology. Sometimes, students earn bachelor's degrees in sociology or education. They may need additional credits in a field of study outside of their major to meet the application requirements for a master's program.[8]

In the United Kingdom, master's program applicants have a wide variety of educational backgrounds. Many applicants have arts-based degrees, but teachers, social workers, and other professionals are also considered.[9]

Graduate Education

Students in master's programs develop their skills in visual art making and learn about theories, approaches, and applications of art therapy practice. They gain skills in facilitating art therapy sessions, administering assessments, and conducting research.

Students are trained to think critically about diversity, equity, and inclusion. This is essential, because most art therapists work cross-culturally.

Graduate programs include experiential and hands-on learning. Typically, in the United States, art therapists-in-training must complete at least 700 supervised internship hours before graduating.[10]

> Wow, that looks like a lot of work!

> It is! But it's worth it!

Registration (United Kingdom)

In the United Kingdom, art therapists must be registered with the Health & Care Professions Council (HCPC) before they can practice. Let's take a look at how this process works.[11]

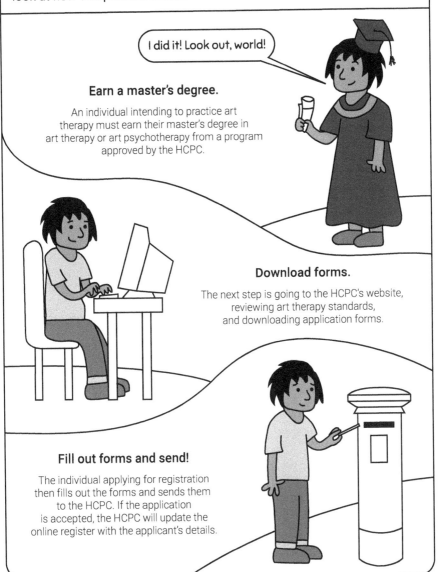

I did it! Look out, world!

Earn a master's degree.

An individual intending to practice art therapy must earn their master's degree in art therapy or art psychotherapy from a program approved by the HCPC.

Download forms.

The next step is going to the HCPC's website, reviewing art therapy standards, and downloading application forms.

Fill out forms and send!

The individual applying for registration then fills out the forms and sends them to the HCPC. If the application is accepted, the HCPC will update the online register with the applicant's details.

Credentials (United States)

National art therapy credentials in the United States are administered by the Art Therapy Credentials Board (ATCB). The process may begin either immediately following the graduate degree, through the ATR-Provisional, or after obtaining post-graduate work experience through the ATR.[12]

ATR-Provisional

Provisional Registered Art Therapist
Individuals can apply for this optional credential after their master's program and after establishing a supervisory relationship with a qualified supervisor.

ATR

Registered Art Therapist
This credential is obtained after completing post-master's supervised work experience.

Credentials (United States)

ATR-BC

Board Certified Art Therapist
This is the highest-level credential for art therapists. It requires passing the national art therapy exam and must be maintained through continuing education.

ATCS

Art Therapy Certified Supervisor
A professional with their ATR-BC may wish to apply for this credential. Obtaining this credential means that the ATCB recognizes their super powers.

Wait a minute...

That's supposed to be **supervision** powers. Basically, individuals with the ATCS have demonstrated proficiency in supervision of student interns and beginning art therapists.

Where Do Art Therapists Work?

The British Association of Art Therapists[13] and the American Art Therapy Association[14] describe the different settings in which art therapists work.

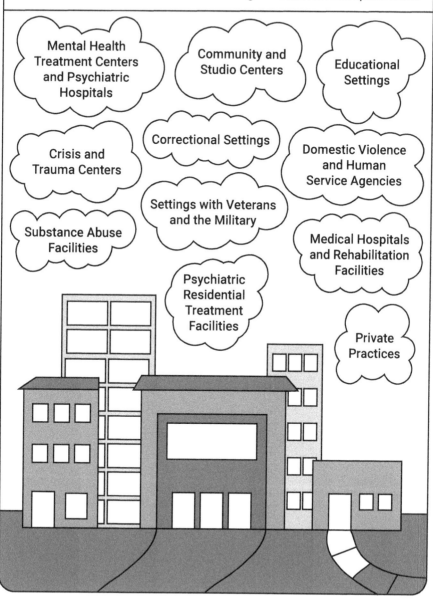

Mental Health Treatment Centers and Psychiatric Hospitals

Community and Studio Centers

Educational Settings

Correctional Settings

Crisis and Trauma Centers

Domestic Violence and Human Service Agencies

Settings with Veterans and the Military

Substance Abuse Facilities

Medical Hospitals and Rehabilitation Facilities

Psychiatric Residential Treatment Facilities

Private Practices

Environment

Art therapists work to maintain a supportive environment for their clients. They must also consider their physical environment and ensure adequate lighting, working surfaces, and organization of materials.[15]

Materials and Media

Art therapists are familiar with art materials and stay informed about new media. Rubin suggested that art therapists fall somewhere on a spectrum in deciding how many art materials to offer to clients.[16] When considering which materials to provide, meeting the clients' needs is most important.

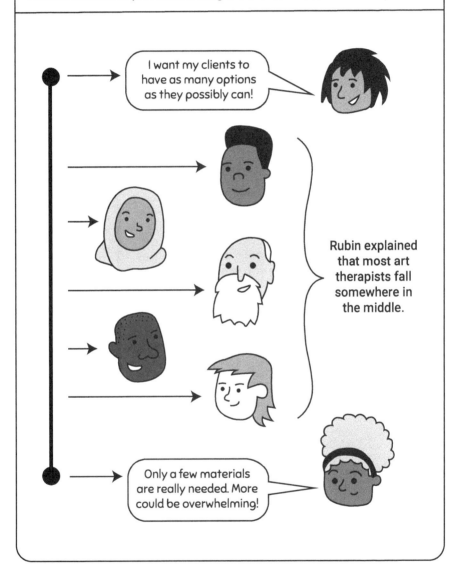

I want my clients to have as many options as they possibly can!

Rubin explained that most art therapists fall somewhere in the middle.

Only a few materials are really needed. More could be overwhelming!

Materials and Media

Art therapists consider the population with which they work before identifying art materials to offer.

Moon explained that personal experiences and social influences affect individuals' associations with art media; no medium is association-free.[17]

Yarn makes me think of my best friend! She is always knitting and crocheting.

Ugh, really? The texture reminds me of spider webs. I hate spiders.

Landgarten wrote that art materials could be conceptualized as being on a continuum.[18]

Least Controlled (Fluid)

Wet Clay · Watercolors · Soft Plasticene · Oil Pastels · Thick Felt Markers · Collage · Hard Plasticene · Thin Felt Markers · Colored Pencils · Lead Pencils

Most Controlled (Rigid)

HEE HEE HEE
HA HA!

Rigid media is likely to support highly cognitive processes, while fluid media may activate affective or libidinal states.

For example, this client appeared to regress when introduced to slippery finger paint.

Materials and Media

What are some materials that art therapists use in practice?[19]

Painting Supplies

Drawing Supplies

Sculpting and Building Materials

Collaging Materials

Recycled and Found Materials

Digital Media

Fiber Materials

Art therapists often consider a specific model, the Expressive Therapies Continuum, to determine which art materials to offer to certain clients. We'll take a closer look in the Framework and Models chapter.

Art Therapy's Evolution as a Profession

Rubin used the metaphor of a garden to illustrate the art therapy profession's beginning, as well as its consistent growth. We will begin this section by displaying the seeds art therapy pioneers planted to establish art therapy as a true profession.[1]

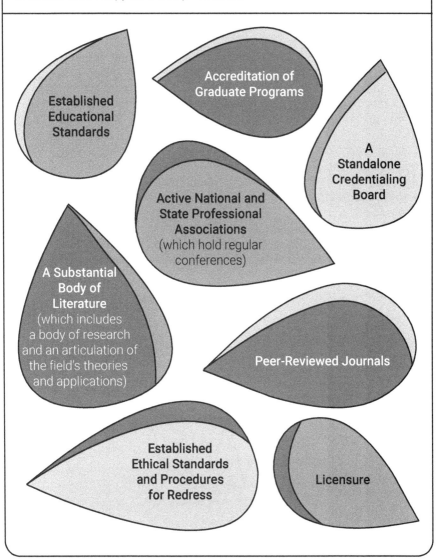

Established Educational Standards

Accreditation of Graduate Programs

A Standalone Credentialing Board

Active National and State Professional Associations (which hold regular conferences)

A Substantial Body of Literature (which includes a body of research and an articulation of the field's theories and applications)

Peer-Reviewed Journals

Established Ethical Standards and Procedures for Redress

Licensure

Fertilizing the Soil

Although the art therapy pioneers planted the seeds of the profession's garden, a few movements and events had to come first to fertilize the soil.

In the late 19th and early 20th century, Freud and Jung popularized the concept of the unconscious. The fascination with dream imagery and inner symbols paved part of the path for art therapy.

Around the same time, some psychiatrists became interested in the art of individuals with mental illnesses. They noted that these individuals appeared to make art in order to cope with their symptoms. It became clear that individuals who had limited verbal capacities benefited from communicating through imagery.[2]

Clinical psychologists began using art tasks for projective testing. "In addition to being attracted to the use of art for the purpose of assessment, it was natural that analytically trained clinicians of all sorts would be drawn to employ it as a means of psychotherapy."[3]

The development of therapeutic art education also fertilized the soil. Educators believed that creative experiences were crucial for healthy development, so they emphasized spontaneous expression over rigid artistic rules.

Planting the Seeds: Literature and Journals

By the 1940s, the soil was properly fertilized and required passionate gardeners to begin planting the seeds.

Margaret Naumburg and Edith Kramer were two of the most prominent figures in growing the profession. Both came from a psychoanalytic background but emphasized different parts of art therapy. While Kramer focused on art processes to enable defenses such as sublimation, Naumburg focused on what she called Dynamically Oriented Art Therapy, in which the art was used in a symbolic, graphic manner.[4]

Adrian Hill was thought to have coined the term art therapy in 1942.[5] Eventually, this became the preferred term for the profession.[6]

Some of the first seeds planted involved professional and research-based writing. For example:

1941–1947 Margaret Naumburg published case studies in psychology journals

1945–1951 Adrian Hill published two books

1950–1956 Margaret Naumburg wrote three books and several book chapters

1958–1979 Edith Kramer wrote three books and multiple seminal articles[7]

1961 Elinor Ulman and Bernard Levy began the first journal, *The Bulletin of Art Therapy*[8] (later called *American Journal of Art Therapy*)

1966 Margaret Naumburg published *Dynamically Oriented Art Therapy*[9]

1973 Scholarly journal: *Art Psychotherapy* (now called *The Arts in Psychotherapy*)[10]

1985 Scholarly journal: *Canadian Art Therapy Association Journal*[11]

1983 Scholarly journal: *Art Therapy: Journal of the American Art Therapy Association*[12]

1996 Scholarly journal: *Inscape* (now called *International Journal of Art Therapy*)[13]

A Substantial Body of Literature

Peer-Reviewed Journals

Planting the Seeds: Education and Accreditation

Over the next two pages, we will track the development of art therapy education and professional associations.[14]

1957   Roger White established the training program at University of Louisville

1964   British Association of Art Therapists was formed

1967   Myra Levick created the program at Hahnemann Medical College (now Drexel University)

1968   A meeting in Philadelphia sparked the American Art Therapy Association

1969   The American Art Therapy Association was formed; Myra Levick was the first president

1969   Wayne Ramirez was the founding president of the Wisconsin Art Therapy Association

1970   The first conference of the American Art Therapy Association was held

1970   Christine Wang served as the Reservations chair for the first AATA conference

1970   Cliff Joseph was part of the founding faculty of the Pratt Institute art therapy program

1971   Elinor Ulman and Bernard Levy began the master's program at George Washington University

1973   The American Art Therapy Association developed educational standards

1973   Helen Landgarten began a training program at Immaculate Heart College that later moved to a master's program at Loyola Marymount University

1973   Robert Ault initiated an art therapy graduate program at Emporia State University

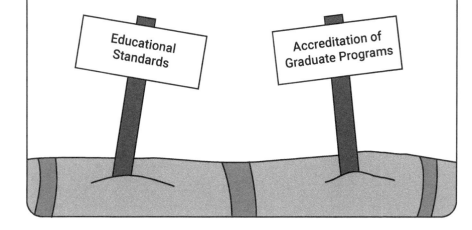

Planting the Seeds: Education and Accreditation

1973 Lucille Venture helped develop the Ad-Hoc Committee to Investigate Encouraging Minority Groups to Enter and Study in the Field of Art Therapy for the American Art Therapy Association

1975 The Education and Training Board (ETB) was created (later called the Education Program Approval Board)

1975 The first programs approved by the ETB were Hahnemann, Loyola Marymount University, George Washington University, and New York State University

1977 Lucille Venture presented her dissertation, *The Black Beat in Art Therapy Experiences*; she was the first in the United States to earn a Ph.D. with a dissertation that emphasized art therapy

1978 Art therapists of color initiated advocacy to emphasize multicultural competency

1981 Harriet Wadeson formed an art therapy program at the University of Illinois, Chicago Circle

1990 Charles Anderson was the founding chairperson of the Mosaic Committee (later the Multicultural Committee)

2003 Harriet Wadeson initiated a post-master's art therapy program at Northwestern University

2009 The American Art Therapy Association listed 33 art therapy programs as approved

2020 The British Association of Art Therapists listed 10 validated art therapy programs

2020 The American Art Therapy Association listed 12 art therapy programs as accredited

Professional Associations

Planting the Seeds: Credentialing and Licensure

The following are some of the important dates in gaining credentialing and licensure for art therapy.[15]

1970   Members of the American Art Therapy Association voted to begin the ATR (Art Therapist, Registered) credential

1993   New Mexico established the first state licensing bill

1993   The Art Therapy Credentialing Board (ATCB) formed to manage the ATR and ATR-BC

1994   As expectations increased, the ATR-BC (Art Therapist, Registered, Board Certified) was created to evidence a higher level of certification

2010   Three states had attained art therapy licensure (separate from other mental health professions): New Mexico, Mississippi, and Kentucky

2020   Washington D.C. and eight states attained specific art therapy licensure: Connecticut, Delaware, New Jersey, New Mexico, Kentucky, Mississippi, Maryland, and Oregon. The following states licensed art therapists under related licenses: New York, Pennsylvania, Texas, Utah, and Wisconsin. Arizona, Louisiana, and New Hampshire recognized art therapists for state hiring and/or title protection

Clinical licensure gives credibility to the profession and helps graduates find employment. Attaining state licensure has proved difficult due to financial and political issues. While some states have obtained licensure specifically for art therapy practice or under a related license, the American Art Therapy Association continues to advocate for regulation of the profession.[16]

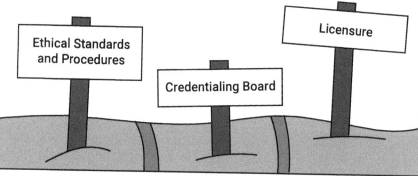

We will check on the growth of the art therapy garden later on! For now, let's check out some developmental models.

Introduction to Framework and Models

This chapter will describe developmental models from multiple theorists. Art therapists should have a strong knowledge of cognitive, emotional, social, and artistic development, so they can see when clients are meeting or deviating from typical development.[1]

Art therapists need to understand human development in order to avoid pathologizing clients and to establish appropriate treatment plans and goals.[2] This applies to all clients, not just children[3] or individuals with developmental disabilities.[4]

Why are there so many models? Couldn't we just use one?

Although developmental perspectives have differences, they all emphasize how people process external experiences.[5] Art therapists can choose between models or integrate them.

Gotcha! So, why do we need to know clients' developmental histories to understand their current problems?

Rubin said, "The very fact that there is an inability to cope with the demands of life in the present means that at some point or other, his development did not proceed in a completely adequate fashion."[6]

Psychosexual Stages

Let's start with a classic developmental model: Sigmund Freud's psychosexual stages.[7]

Oral Phase (0–1 year)

Individuals are most concerned with getting fed.

Anal Phase (1–3 years)

The focus shifts to toileting, toddling, and talking.
In this phase, it is important for parenting to be supportive and positive.

I go potty!

Phallic Phase (3–6 years)

Individuals may think about marrying the parent of the opposite sex, but they realize they are already spoken for. Individuals then align with the same-sex parent.

Dad is so fun! I want to marry him! But wait, Mom is married to him.

Psychosexual Stages

Latency Phase (7–11 years)

Individuals move away from being closely attached to family.

I like my family, but my friends are becoming more and more important!

Genital Phase (12+ years)

Individuals begin to shift from narcissism to caring about other people.

Mahler Stages

Mahler's developmental model focuses on the first three years of life. In this theory, the child is oriented through the mother.[8]

Symbiosis
Age 0–5 Months

The infant is focused solely on themselves. The infant is unaware of being separate from their mother.

In this stage, mother and child use "mutual cueing"— a preverbal means of communication.

> Oh, you're so cute!

> I'm just looking out for number one, that's me.

> I'm becoming my own man, but I'm still a big fan of Mom.

Separation/Individuation
Age 5–24 Months

The child increasingly sees the mother as an individual separate from themselves. The child begins to establish their own identity, though this is a lifelong process.

Separation/Individuation is divided into three substages. Let's take a look at those on the next couple of pages.

Mahler Stages

Rapprochement
Age 14–24 Months

The toddler realizes that they are an independent person separate from mother, which is both exciting and scary. Behaviors may alternate between running off to explore the environment and being clingy.

The child may exhibit a play behavior known as "shadowing and darting away" in which they cling to mother, then run off, usually with a look back over their shoulder as an invitation to play or to confirm her ongoing presence.

The ego defense of splitting evolves in early childhood—the child is unable to conceptualize the object (mother) as containing opposite presentations (cuddling and nurturing as well as angry and yelling).

Consolidation of Individuality and Emotional Object Constancy
Age 24–36 Months

The child can create a mental image of their mother to provide comfort when she is not around. Individuals in this stage have a distinct personality and their separation anxiety tends to dissolve.

Erikson's Psychosocial Stages

Erik Erikson[9] expanded on Freud's psychosexual stages and identified eight stages of typical development. For each stage, Erikson noted two conflicting concepts that individuals resolve to become well-adjusted and successful members of society. Individuals do not need to complete a stage in order to move to the next one.

A guide to the terms used

Virtue: The concept that individuals learn upon successful management of the stage.
Maladaption: A trait that develops when the individual's caregiver is too involved.
Malignancy: A trait that develops when the individual's caregiver is neglectful or negative.

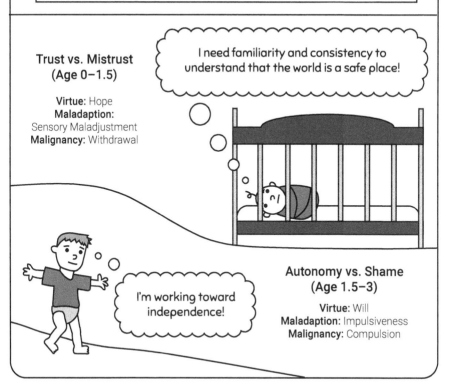

Trust vs. Mistrust (Age 0–1.5)

Virtue: Hope
Maladaption: Sensory Maladjustment
Malignancy: Withdrawal

I need familiarity and consistency to understand that the world is a safe place!

I'm working toward independence!

Autonomy vs. Shame (Age 1.5–3)

Virtue: Will
Maladaption: Impulsiveness
Malignancy: Compulsion

Erikson's Psychosocial Stages

I'm learning moral consequences and understanding limits while discovering what I can accomplish!

Initiative vs. Guilt (Age 3–5)

Virtue: Purpose
Maladaption: Ruthlessness
Malignancy: Inhibition

Industry vs. Inferiority (Age 5–12)

Virtue: Competency
Maladaption: Narrow Virtuosity
Malignancy: Inertia

I'm learning how to achieve in school, but sometimes I feel like I'm not as good as the other kids. I need encouragement from my parents and teachers!

Societal standards and the opinions of my peer group are becoming increasingly important, which leads me to the question...

Who am I?

Identity vs. Role Confusion (Age 12–20)

Virtue: Fidelity
Maladaption: Fanaticism
Malignancy: Repudiation

Erikson's Psychosocial Stages

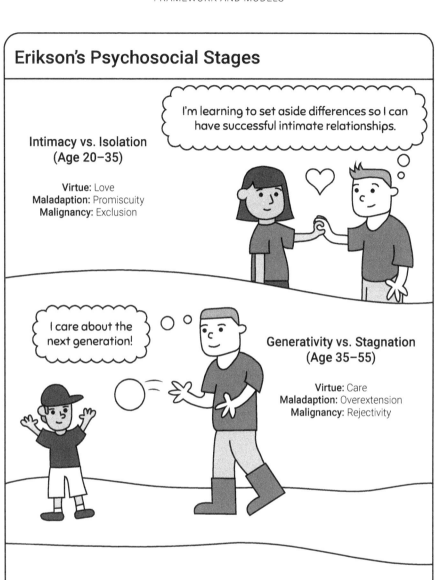

Intimacy vs. Isolation (Age 20–35)

Virtue: Love
Maladaption: Promiscuity
Malignancy: Exclusion

I'm learning to set aside differences so I can have successful intimate relationships.

I care about the next generation!

Generativity vs. Stagnation (Age 35–55)

Virtue: Care
Maladaption: Overextension
Malignancy: Rejectivity

Ego Integrity vs. Despair (Age 55+)

Virtue: Wisdom
Maladaption: Presumption
Malignancy: Disdain

I feel good about what I've accomplished in my life.

Piaget's Stages of Cognitive Development

Jean Piaget[10] studied individuals' mental processes and cognitive development. He theorized that intellectual growth occurs when one adapts to their external world. Piaget identified four stages in typical development.

Sensorimotor Stage (Birth to 18 Months)

In this stage, individuals learn through their senses and reflexes and actively manipulate materials. One main accomplishment during this stage is understanding object permanence; the individual understands that an object exists, even when they can no longer see it.

Oh no, I'm late for work.

Preoperational Stage (18 Months to Age 6)

In the preoperational stage, individuals form ideas based on their perceptions. They can typically only focus on one variable at a time and tend to overgeneralize. Individuals are likely to engage in animistic thinking, in which they believe that animals have thoughts and feelings.

Piaget's Stages of Cognitive Development

Concrete Operational Stage
(Age 6 to Age 12)

Individuals form their ideas based on logical reasoning and limit their thinking to familiar objects and events. Individuals achieve seriation, in which they can organize and classify items.

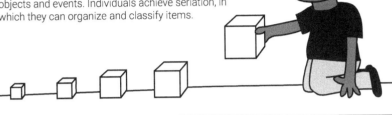

Formal Operational Stage (Age 12+)

In this stage, individuals are able to think conceptually and hypothetically. They are prone to the "imaginary audience" in which they think everyone is looking at them, as well as the "personal fable" in which they believe the rules don't apply to them.

Everyone's looking at my giant zit!

Lowenfeld Stages of Drawing Development

Viktor Lowenfeld researched graphic indicators of development and identified six stages.[11] The stages do not begin at exactly the same age for everyone, but they provide a guideline for what to expect in typical child development. **It is important not to use these stages to diagnose any specific child or to compare one child to another.**

The Scribbling Stage | Typically Age 2

The kinesthetic quality of drawing is the most important characteristic of this stage. The act of scribbling starts out disorganized but becomes more orderly as this stage draws to a close.

The Preschematic Stage | Typically Ages 3 and 4

This stage is characterized by the first conscious creation of form. Typically, the first representational form drawn is a person, represented by a circle and two vertical lines. Children continue to experiment and create new forms. Objects appear to float around the page.

Lowenfeld Stages of Drawing Development

The Schematic Stage | Typically Age 6

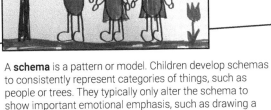

A **schema** is a pattern or model. Children develop schemas to consistently represent categories of things, such as people or trees. They typically only alter the schema to show important emotional emphasis, such as drawing a much larger foot after having hurt their foot.

In this stage, children tend to draw everything lined up on a base line.

The Gang Stage: The Dawning Realism
Typically Ages 8–10

In this stage, children learn that schemas do not accurately represent reality. Children begin adding more details and start rendering overlapping objects and multiple horizon lines or planes to indicate dimensional space. Children may become critical of their work as they begin comparing themselves to others.

Lowenfeld Stages of Drawing Development

The Pseudo-Naturalistic Stage | Typically Age 12

Individuals become even more critical of their work and shift their focus to creating technically accurate or esthetically appealing products. They may start experimenting with shading and depicting motion, along with creating three-dimensional depth. Some individuals may prefer to make cartoons or caricatures.

The Period of Decision | Typically Ages 14–16

At this stage, individuals must make a conscious decision to learn and practice drawing skills in order for graphic development to continue. Individuals may begin to experiment with different art media and become skilled at more expressive rather than realistic styles.

Rubin Stages of Artistic Development

Rubin[12] expanded upon Lowenfeld's stages due to their lack of applicability for painting and three-dimensional media. Rubin identified the following stages of artistic development. As with all other developmental models, the ages listed are merely guidelines! Every individual is different, and these stages typically overlap.[13]

Manipulating (1–2 years)

In this stage, sensory and kinesthetic qualities of creating are most important. Individuals are beginning to focus on what is made, but there is very little concern with the finished product.

Forming (2–3 years)

Individuals gain more control over materials and increase repetition to demonstrate their level of control. They create Gestalts, which are "separate shapes or objects which have existence of their own."[14]

Naming (3–4 years)

Children begin to name their marks and objects, even though, to an adult, they don't look much like what they're attempting to represent.

Rubin Stages of Artistic Development

Representing (4–6 years)

Individuals typically create based on their interests. Children's creations begin to look like what they're trying to represent. They learn to control their impulses and experiment with a variety of ways to represent the same thing.

Consolidating (6–9 years)

Children discover their preferred ways of representing objects. They begin to shift from egocentric to social views.

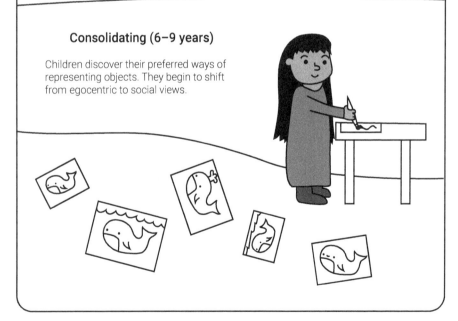

Rubin Stages of Artistic Development

Naturalizing (9–12 years)

Children begin to create with more realistic proportions and accurate spatial relationships. In this stage, children become more critical of their artwork.

Personalizing (12–18 years)

If individuals are successful in the naturalizing stage, they become very skilled at creating realistic representations. Individuals who struggled may turn to crafts or abstract art. Individuals begin to explore their own styles and become increasingly critical about the quality of artwork they produce.

Golomb's Model of Child Art Development

Arnheim's law of differentiation explains that drawing development starts out simple and becomes more complex in two ways.

Addition of Details   **Transformations of the Original**

Claire Golomb[15] expanded on this theory, as well as the work of Viktor Lowenfeld. She noted that children work out solutions...

According to the nature of the medium   Using inherent visual logic   Based on their level of satisfaction with the outcome

According to Golomb, creative development depends on the child's experience with the medium, level of interest, ability to monitor actions, and willingness to revise their work.

Expressive Therapies Continuum

Sandra Kagin and Vija Lusebrink developed the Expressive Therapies Continuum, or ETC, in 1978.[16] This model consists of four levels that represent creative functioning. The ETC is useful to art therapists when they are deciding the most appropriate media for their clients.

Kagin and Lusebrink conceptualized the framework hierarchically, much like this:

CR

Each bar represents a different level in the hierarchy. Each horizontal level is made up of two components.

C — **Sy**

Cognitive Component   Symbolic Component

Most complex form of creative functioning

P — **A**

Perceptual Component   Affective Component

K — **S**

Kinesthetic Component   Sensory Component

Most basic form of creative functioning

The components were placed on either the left or right side to indicate which hemisphere of the brain is responsible for each component.[17]

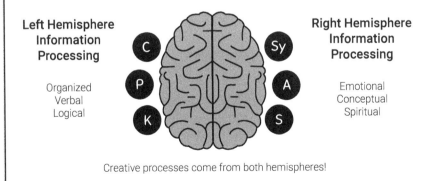

Left Hemisphere Information Processing

Organized
Verbal
Logical

Right Hemisphere Information Processing

Emotional
Conceptual
Spiritual

Creative processes come from both hemispheres!

Expressive Therapies Continuum

What are the levels? Let's start with the most basic.[18]

Kinesthetic/Sensory Level

This level involves movement and sensory experience. The emphasis is on the kinesthetic process, not the finished product.

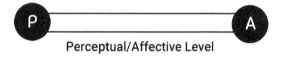

Perceptual/Affective Level

Here the focus on kinesthetic process has shifted to creating a product representative of the individual's perceptions about the world. Emotion comes into play during art making, as well.

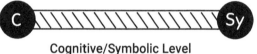

Cognitive/Symbolic Level

The cognitive/symbolic level involves sophisticated information processing. Individuals use symbols to represent thoughts and feelings. Individuals consciously plan and problem-solve to complete artwork.

CR

The vertical bar symbolizes the creative level, or a wholeness in the creative process. This level occurs at any development level or when all levels integrate.

All levels may come into play when reaching the creative level. It may be more helpful to think of the model this way.[19]

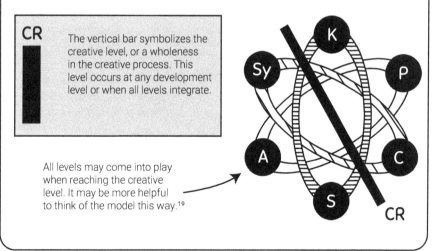

Expressive Therapies Continuum

Art materials often correlate to the components in the ETC. For example:

K

Kinesthetic

Media for physical movement:

**Clay
Yarn
Paint**

Of course, this is not an exhaustive list!

S

Sensory

Media for sensory experiences:

**Scented Markers
Oil Pastels
Finger Paint**

P

Perceptual

Media for containment:

**Small Paper
Trays or Frames
Metal**

A

Affective

Media to give form to feelings:

**Chalk Pastels
Poster Paint
Watercolor Paint**

Most art materials fit into more than one component!

C

Cognitive

Highly structured media for planning:

**Pencil
Wood
Digital Media**

Sy

Symbolic

Media for symbol formation:

**Pen and Ink
Collage Images
Assemblage**

Art therapists can use the ETC to identify which levels clients prefer and which levels they have blocked. With this information, art therapists can better determine which materials and experiences will be therapeutic.[20]

Developmental Art Therapy

Art therapists may look to some of the models presented in this chapter to compare clients' cognitive and creative development with typical human development. By understanding typical milestones, therapists can intervene when individuals are not meeting them.[21]

Williams and Woods divided the process of art therapy into four developmental stages:[22]

Stage 1: Art materials should entice and stimulate the clients. In this stage, the art therapist is directive.

Stage 2: Art making should enhance clients' self-esteem, their ability to manipulate, and their conceptual skills. The art therapist is available to redirect and reassure the individual when needed.

Stage 3: In this stage, children respond to limitations and expectations. The art therapist provides suggestions to enhance motivation and manage the clients' behavior.

Stage 4: Art making emphasizes clients' unique personalities. Art therapists are present to provide support and set limits as needed.

In general, art making is an avenue for individuals to learn and strengthen new skills that can help reach developmental goals.[23]

Art therapists work from a variety of approaches that lay the groundwork for their practice. Let's take a look at some of these

Theories and Approaches

Introduction to Theories and Approaches

Rubin stated that "it would probably be accurate to say that if truth be told, there have always been as many different approaches as there are art therapists."[1] Although each art therapist has their own style of working, specific theoretical orientations lay the groundwork. The following are some of the most prominent theories and approaches in the field.[2]

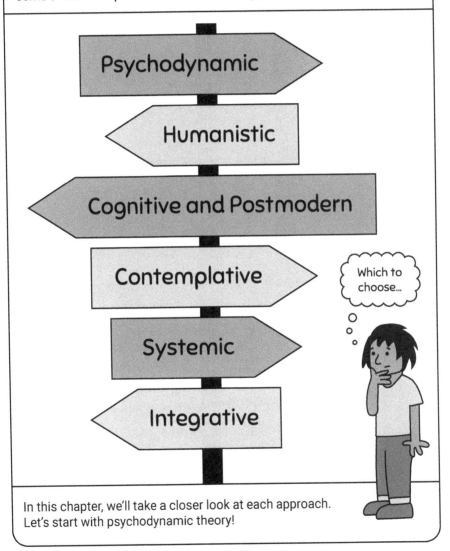

In this chapter, we'll take a closer look at each approach. Let's start with psychodynamic theory!

Psychodynamic Approaches

We will briefly discuss three approaches under the psychodynamic umbrella: Freudian, Jungian, and object relations approaches.[3]

Psychodynamic

Key goals for psychodynamic approaches:[4]

Freudian

Making the unconscious conscious
Reducing the influence of the id by strengthening the ego

Jungian

Transforming personality
Accessing inner wisdom

Object Relations

Improving relationships with others

Freudian Theory

Sigmund Freud was the originator of psychoanalysis. Freud believed in the importance of making the unconscious conscious. But what exactly is the unconscious?[5]

The image of an iceberg is a common symbol to represent the three levels of the mind.

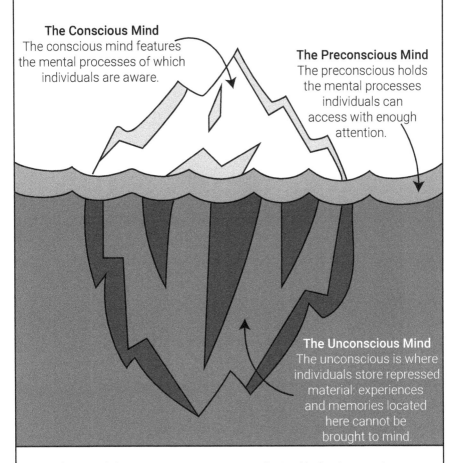

The Conscious Mind
The conscious mind features the mental processes of which individuals are aware.

The Preconscious Mind
The preconscious holds the mental processes individuals can access with enough attention.

The Unconscious Mind
The unconscious is where individuals store repressed material: experiences and memories located here cannot be brought to mind.

Freud believed the unconscious causes undesired behaviors, as it stores unresolved emotional conflict. By making the unconscious accessible, the therapist can help clients better understand their behaviors.

Therapeutic Relationship

Therapists who practice from psychodynamic approaches are likely to remain as neutral as possible and rarely disclose personal information to the client. This "blank screen" approach encourages clients to unconsciously associate the therapist with a significant person in their lives; this association can then be analyzed therapeutically.[6]

This would be a good time to introduce the terms transference and countertransference.

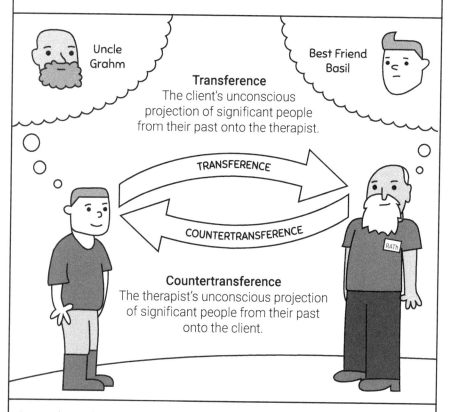

Uncle Grahm

Best Friend Basil

Transference
The client's unconscious projection of significant people from their past onto the therapist.

TRANSFERENCE

COUNTERTRANSFERENCE

Countertransference
The therapist's unconscious projection of significant people from their past onto the client.

In psychoanalytic approaches, transference is typically seen as beneficial. When the source of transference becomes conscious, clients can have a better understanding of their past experiences and can therefore work to effectively resolve them.

Free Association

Free association involves encouraging the client to verbalize whatever comes to mind. Freud believed this process made it possible to access repressed material locked in the unconscious.[7]

Margaret Naumburg, an art therapy pioneer, combined Freud's theory with art making.[8]

Naumburg believed the unconscious could be accessed through spontaneous creation, in a similar manner to free association.[9]

Interpretation

Freud also believed that dreams were avenues to tap into the unconscious. The therapist's job is to explain the meaning of the person's behaviors in their dreams. Studying the symbols found in dreams is particularly important in dream analysis.

By interpreting unconscious material from dreams, free associations, and transference relationships, the ego can then assimilate new material and therefore continue uncovering more material.[10]

Margaret Naumburg believed that the intention had to come from the artist; she was skeptical of simplified versions of interpretation.[11]

The Three Structures of the Psyche

In Freud's theory, the psyche, or one's personality, is broken up into three separate parts: the id, the ego, and the superego. Each part forms at a different stage of development.[12]

The Id

Freud considered the id as the primitive part of the personality that seeks immediate satisfaction or pleasure. The id does not consider social norms or consequences when acting.

It might be helpful to picture the id as an infant or toddler, because children in those developmental stages typically act on impulses.

The Ego

The ego is the component of the psyche that uses reason to make decisions. It takes into account the impulsive desires of the id along with societal expectations in the real world before acting.

This is a sensible gentleman who could represent the ego.

The Superego

The superego's focus is on the values of society. It attempts to control the id's impulses through the conscience and increase the ego's expectations through the ideal self, or an imagined but perfect version of oneself.

This person clearly has strong social values and high standards.

Defense Mechanisms

Defense mechanisms[13] are unconscious ways to avoid negative or unpleasant feelings. In psychoanalytic terms, they are ways the ego protects against id impulses. These can be difficult to understand, so let's add ice cream to the picture. That makes it fun, right?

Repression

Repression involves keeping negative thoughts tucked away in the unconscious.

This is the worst thing that could have happened to me. Without even knowing it, I will bury this so deep into my psyche that I will never consciously remember it.

You know that has a lot of fat and sugar, right?

Nah, this is good for me!

Denial

Denial occurs when one is blind to the reality of a situation.

You're the one who wants to get ice cream.

Uh...what?

Projection

Projection involves attributing one's own thoughts, emotions, or actions to someone else.

Defense Mechanisms

Displacement

Displacement occurs when one uses a substitute to act out an impulse.

Regression

Regression involves going back to a previous developmental stage.

Sublimation

Sublimation occurs when one channels an unacceptable impulse into a socially acceptable behavior.

REMEMBER

These are simplified examples to help demonstrate the defense mechanisms. Keep in mind that these occur unconsciously![14]

Freudian Art Therapy

Edith Kramer emphasized the utilization of sublimation in art therapy. By engaging in the creative process, one is likely to experience what Kramer called "artistic sublimation."[15]

This is when an individual participates in the socially productive behavior of art making and thereby avoids succumbing to their id's impulses.

Freudian art therapists encourage clients to participate in open-ended art tasks and use questions to help the individual free associate.[16]

Art therapy also makes use of Freud's "pleasure principle," in which people inherently seek out pleasure and avoid pain. Art is often a pleasurable experience, so art therapy is beneficial in this way.

Psychoanalytic Art Therapy

The following case[17] is about a client who was experiencing anxiety and depression, which were affecting her confidence in raising her children. By using a psychoanalytic approach, the art therapist encouraged her to choose what art materials to work with as well as what to make. After creating, the client made associations with the art product.

In the first session, the client painted red flowers.

Throughout her sessions, she became comfortable with making associations with her art products. Her artwork and self-discovery led to increased insight. For example...

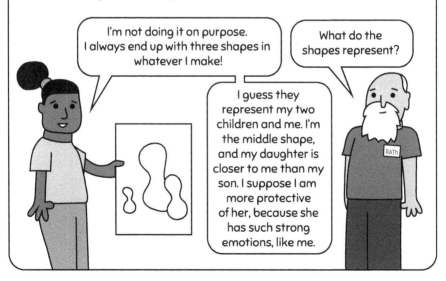

Object Relations Theory

Object relations theory[18] emphasizes individuals' relationships and early attachment. Theorists recognize that people's relationships with others affect their personalities.

In object relations approaches, therapists provide a "holding environment," a term coined by Donald Winnicott. This means that therapists provide a comfortable space for clients to experience personal growth.[19]

The objects in object relations theory are what people put their energy into. The object may be a person or item that satisfies a need.

Transitional Space and Objects

Winnicott described transitional spaces and transitional objects.[20]

Transitional Space

A metaphorical space where inner and outer realities merge.

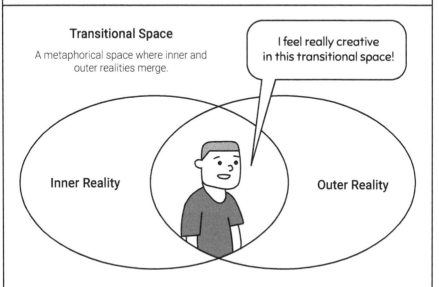

Art making can become a transitional space, as it combines ones subjective and objective experiences.

Transitional Object

A tangible object that holds special value; it is symbolic of an important figure in the owner's life. The item helps one move from dependence to independence.

Malchiodi stated, "Art products can become transitional objects...imbued with meaning beyond what they are in reality."[21]

Jungian Theory

Carl Jung developed analytic psychology.[22] Much like Freud, he believed in the importance of addressing the unconscious. However, Jung's model of the unconscious was slightly different. Let's look at that iceberg again.

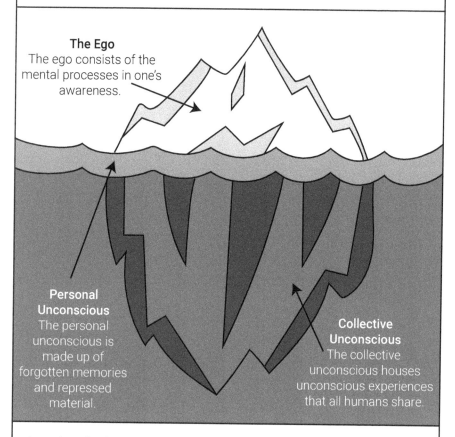

The Ego
The ego consists of the mental processes in one's awareness.

Personal Unconscious
The personal unconscious is made up of forgotten memories and repressed material.

Collective Unconscious
The collective unconscious houses unconscious experiences that all humans share.

Jung thought that most individuals reevaluate their behaviors and values at midlife, so this stage of life became an emphasis in analytic psychology. Jung believed that individuals are constantly developing and that humans' past and future affect their present personalities.

Jung believed individuation was one of the most important goals of therapy. We will define this process on the next page.

Archetypes

Archetypes[23] are innate patterns of being that are timeless and universal across cultures. Jung posited that the archetypes reside in a deep layer of the psyche which he called the collective unconscious. Jung thought that many archetypes existed, but there are four he emphasized in his therapeutic approach.

The Persona

The persona is how we present ourselves to other people. It may be helpful to think of the persona as the mask we put on when interacting with people we don't know well.

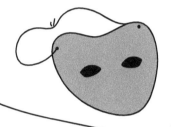

The Anima/Animus

The anima consists of the feminine aspects in the male psyche.

The animus consists of the masculine aspects in the female psyche.

The Self

The self is the cohesive unit of the unconscious and the conscious. Individuation, the process by which all aspects of personality are integrated, is driven by the self and realizes its full potential.

The Shadow

The shadow is the archetype that holds all the aspects of the self deemed unacceptable (by society and by the individual).

Archetypes

Each individual's personality is likely to be shaped by several archetypes, though one may play a dominant role at any given time. The following are a few more examples of archetypes that have the potential to become activated in a person's psyche. Jung believed we are each born with a unique blueprint featuring certain archetypes.[24]

Directed and Nondirected Thinking

Jung identified two ways of thinking: directed and nondirected.[25]

Directed

Directed thinking involves linear processes that are grounded in reality. Thoughts are organized and may revolve around a specific goal.

I am waiting for the bus so I can go to the grocery store. Once I arrive at the store, I will buy noodles, cheese, butter, and milk. I will then go home and cook macaroni and cheese by following a recipe. Finally, I will consume the delicious meal.

Nondirected

Nondirected thinking involves fantastical and spontaneous processes. This type of thinking is more likely to conjure imagery and is akin to daydreaming.

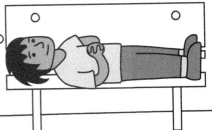

Active Imagination and Psychic Energy

Jung suggested that individuals can develop the relationship between the conscious and unconscious components of one's psyche by utilizing active imagination.[26] In this process, individuals focus their attention on inner symbols by expressing themselves through creative activities.[27]

Jung believed that psychic energy consists of an individual's emotions and instincts. This energy has the ability to move between the conscious and unconscious and therefore has a healing quality; Jung believed that healing occurs when the conscious and unconscious are balanced.[28]

By creating imagery and engaging in creative activities, one utilizes psychic energy and can therefore experience personal growth.

Jungian Art Therapy

Jung utilized painting with his clients to help them tap into the unconscious and enhance their self-awareness.[29] He believed that interpreting dreams and participating in creative activities helps to confront the unconscious. Jungian art therapists have adopted these perspectives in their work with clients.

Art therapists are likely to help individuals use metaphor and symbolic imagery to better understand their unconscious material and the self.

Humanistic Approaches

Humanistic

Let's talk about three different humanistic approaches: person–centered, existential, and Gestalt!

Key goals for humanistic approaches:[30]

Person-Centered

Trusting oneself
Coping with problems

Existential

Realizing one's full potential
Living authentically

Gestalt

Increasing self-awareness
Integrating all aspects of oneself

Humanistic Theories

Moon suggested that humanistic theories typically work under the following assumptions.[31]

Person-Centered Theory

Carl Rogers developed person-centered or client-centered therapy.[32] When compared with psychodynamic approaches, person-centered therapy is typically more nondirective.

Rogers believed the major goal of therapy is for individuals to become more independent and confident in their lives.

Other goals of person-centered therapy include...

• Gaining the ability to trust oneself

• Developing a willingness to continue growing and changing

• Finding effective ways to cope with problems

• Opening oneself to new experiences

The Therapeutic Relationship

Carl Rogers asserted that the relationship between client and therapist is the most important aspect of therapy; the alliance holds more significance than any techniques or interventions.[33]

To enhance the therapeutic relationship, person-centered therapists typically exhibit...

> I think we've had similar experiences. I could share some of these with you, if you'd like.

> Your openness makes me feel like a normal human. Sure!

Congruence

Demonstrating openness and being one's genuine self.

Unconditional Positive Regard

Accepting the client under any circumstances.

> This therapist must think I'm a real dummy.

> This client is worthy and capable.

Empathic Understanding

Acknowledging and comprehending the client's inner world.

> That sounds really exhausting!

> Everything in my life just feels exhausting.

The therapeutic relationship may be further developed through active listening, in which the therapist puts complete focus on what the client is discussing.[34]

Self-Direction

One of the main assumptions in person-centered therapy is that all clients have the ability to self-direct and solve their own problems. Individuals are responsible for making positive changes in their lives.[35]

Clients identify their own goals in therapy; it is therefore the therapist's job to create an environment where individuals can experience growth.[36]

The therapeutic process is considered a shared journey, in which the therapist enters a client's world to assist them in meeting their goals and working toward self-actualization.

Maslow's Hierarchy

Abraham Maslow postulated that all individuals need to have certain needs met before they are able to reach self-actualization.[37] In self-actualization, individuals recognize and meet their full potential.

Maslow's hierarchy is typically seen as a pyramid, in which the most basic needs are located at the bottom. Once needs from one section are met, individuals can move up to the next level. If some needs are unmet, all the other needs tend to get put on the back burner.

The needs are structured as follows:

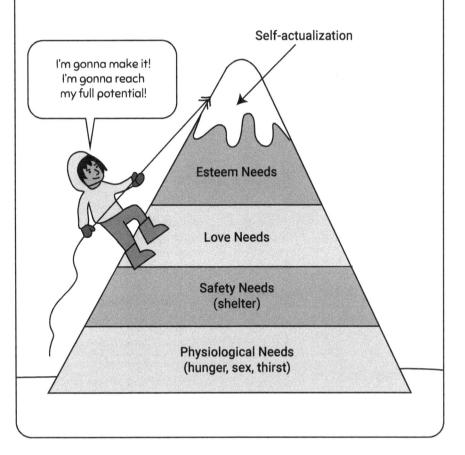

Seven Stages of Therapy

Rogers described seven stages in clients' typical attitudes and behaviors throughout the therapeutic process.[38]

Stage One

Resisting change

I don't even know why I'm here.

Stage Two

Discussing others or external experiences

My family is really driving me nuts!

Stage Three

Talking about themselves without ownership

I've always been this way.

Stage Four

Describing personal emotions

I'm feeling anxious right now.

Stage Five

Taking responsibility for actions

I really messed that situation up, but I think I can improve it.

Stage Six

Becoming more honest with themselves and others

I'm feeling much better about my relationship with my family.

Stage Seven

Demonstrating empathy and self-actualization

I have a better understanding of how my comments have made others feel.

Person-Centered Expressive Arts Therapy

Carl Rogers' daughter, Natalie Rogers, built on her father's work by including expressive arts in therapy. She believed that making art in the presence of a therapist helps create a closer and more genuine relationship. Rogers believed that creating art is a form of communication.[39]

Bruce Moon noted that communication through art making is crucial in obtaining more information about the client's experiences.[40]

Person-centered art therapists are likely to acknowledge...

Person-Centered Art Therapy

The following case[41] is about a client who was experiencing depression. She expressed interest in attending group art therapy sessions to learn art techniques, but she did not want to talk about her emotions. The art therapist encouraged her to come to the art room.

The client participated in guided imagery and art making once a week. In the first session, the art therapist asked if the client wanted to share her artwork; the client explained that she did not know what to say. The art therapist suggested taking some time to reflect on the painting and writing whatever came to mind.

Hesitantly at first, the client began writing on the back of all of her paintings. Her series of landscapes became an outlet to express her loneliness and hopelessness. Through her artwork and writing, she gradually revealed her grief from the deaths of her husband and son.

After ten sessions, the client brought in an image of Panama Beach as a reference photo. The client mentioned that this was the location of the last vacation she had taken with her son, and she wanted to make a memorial piece. After completing the landscape, the client wrote about how much she missed her son.

Through art making, the client could explore the painful events from her past and could safely process her emotions.

Existential Theory[42]

Existential therapy aims to help individuals experience authentic lives. Much like the previous humanistic theories, one of the most important goals is to increase self-awareness. Through enhanced awareness, one can reach their full potential.

Existential theory asserts that human existence does not have to be predetermined or fixed; by making choices and changes, we can continue to recreate ourselves.

There are two aspects of existential therapy that require balance.

Acknowledging limitations — Recognizing life's possibilities

"Life is kind of tricky."

Existential therapy emphasizes the importance of a genuine therapeutic relationship. Through this relationship, therapists assist clients in identifying and accepting their life's responsibilities. Therapists also demonstrate congruence for modeling purposes. If these concepts sound familiar, it's because they are also valued in person-centered therapy!

Universal Experiences

Existential therapists typically rely less on specific techniques or interventions and more on the underlying philosophy that guides their practice. Therapists consider humankind's universal experiences and how they affect individuals.[43]

Some of these universal experiences include:

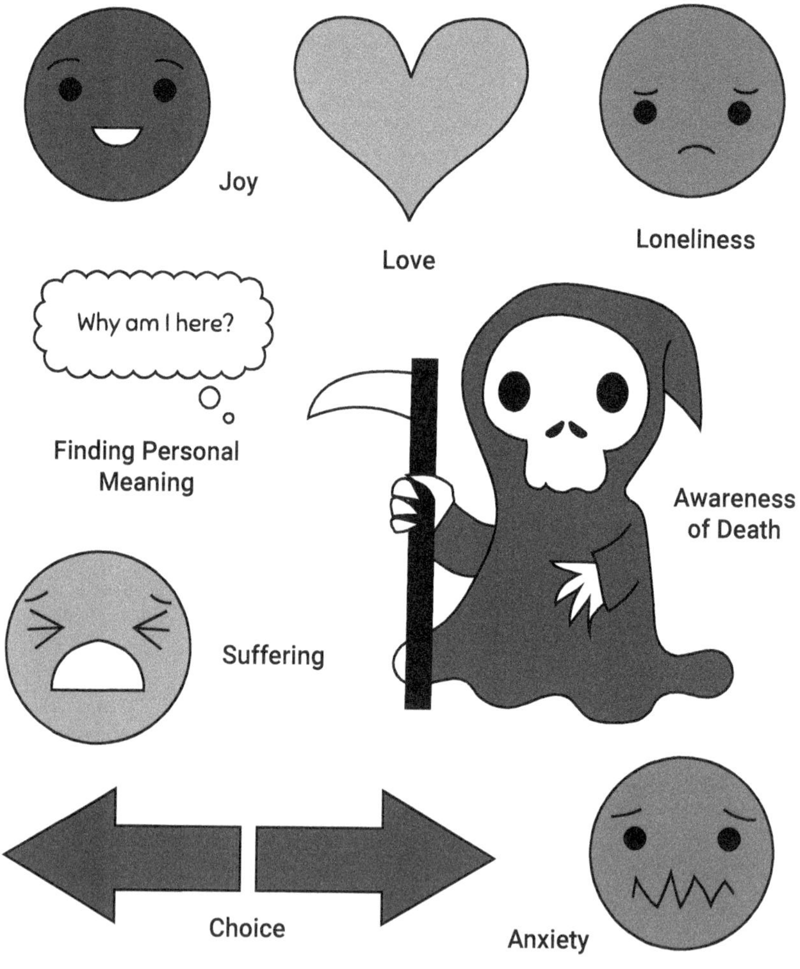

Joy

Love

Loneliness

Why am I here?

Finding Personal Meaning

Awareness of Death

Suffering

Choice

Anxiety

Dimensions

Corey listed these dimensions of existential therapy:[44]

The capacity for self-awareness

Developing goals and motivations.

Freedom and responsibility

Being responsible for one's own actions; having control over one's life through the choices they make.

Creating one's identity and forming meaningful relationships

Evaluating how other people have affected their personalities; recognizing that humans are interdependent.

Dimensions

Anxiety as a living condition

Anxiety stems from the need to survive or indicates personal growth. Anxiety typically reduces as clients gain more positive elements in their lives.

Normal anxiety
An appropriate response to the situation.

Neurotic anxiety
A response that is out of proportion compared to the situation.

That's a lot of dishes to do in very little time. If I do them quickly, I think I can finish before my guests get here.

Look at all those dishes! I'll never get them done, and my guests will think I'm gross!

Awareness of death and nonbeing

Individuals understand that they will eventually die and therefore learn to enjoy the present.[45]

I mean, yeah, I'll die like everyone else, but ping pong sure quells my existential dread.

Search for Meaning

Existential therapists are likely to address the "search for meaning" by asking clients if they like where they are heading in life or how their identity is being formed. Therapists believe clients are responsible for creating their own meaning through their personal value system.

Viktor Frankl coined the term "existential vacuum," which essentially means the inability to find meaning in one's life. Individuals are affected by the thought of eventually dying and do not bother engaging in meaningful activities. Therapists help find new meaning in clients' lives through logotherapy.[46]

Existential Art Therapy

Art making gives clients the opportunity to make choices and work toward a positive self-direction. "The art process serves as a stage for therapist-client dialog about existential issues of freedom to choose, will to meaning, and the search for purpose, values, and goals."[47]

The emphasis is typically on breaking barriers that keep individuals from living to their full potential. Malchiodi noted that creative work is helpful in this sense, because it "offers free choice and opportunity to make sense of what often seems senseless or meaningless."[48]

The following case[49] involves a client who regularly participated in an art therapy group in a hospital. In one session, the art therapist began with a story and encouraged the group members to respond to the tale through their artwork.

Existential Art Therapy

The client was in the hospital due to a car accident. She was a full-time student and lived in her parents' house. She displayed resistance to moving out and experienced significant anxiety whenever the topic was brought up.

She considered the story and began making an art response.

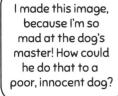

I made this image, because I'm so mad at the dog's master! How could he do that to a poor, innocent dog?

After some thought, the client realized that her rage toward the dog's master correlated with her relationship with her parents. Her parents had never abused her, but they had overindulged her and enabled her dependence on them. In a way, her parents had never allowed her to grow up.

In this session, the client set aside her resistance and began to process her living situation.

Gestalt Theory

Fritz Perls is the founder of Gestalt therapy.[50] When using a Gestalt approach, the therapist assumes that clients can confront their problems. Gestalt therapists help clients work toward experiencing the present moment, as well as increasing self-awareness. Therapists make sure they are genuine with their clients.

Gestalt approaches feature the following aspects.

Integration
Clients work to achieve balance between themselves and their environments. They connect with the parts of themselves they would prefer to reject and develop new strategies to navigate the world around them.[51]

YOU ARE HERE

Here and Now
The emphasis is on the present space and moment, rather than focusing on the client's history or events that occur outside of therapy. The therapeutic relationship or group creates a social microcosm that brings clients' interpersonal skills to light so dysfunctional patterns can be identified and addressed.[52]

Internal Support
Gestalt therapists help individuals move from external to internal sources of support.

Environmental Factors
There is a dynamic relationship between individuals and their environments.

Gestalt Therapy

When compared with the other humanistic approaches, Gestalt therapists tend to be a little more active in the therapeutic process. Even so, the focus is on taking the client's lead and experiencing the client fully through genuine contact.[53] Therapist and client are companions on the therapeutic journey.[54]

Gestalt therapists help clients resolve "unfinished business."

Unfinished business is comprised of events or relationships in their past in which the client has not achieved closure. When individuals have unfinished business, they find it difficult to experience the present moment.

Resistances to Contact

Gestalt therapists believe that contact—that is, interacting with one's external environment—is crucial for positive change. Individuals develop resistances to contact in order to cope with stressful events, but resistances also stop them from fully experiencing life.[55] Polster and Polster described the following ways that individuals resist contact.[56]

Principles

Corey noted the following principles of Gestalt therapy.[58]

Holism
The whole person is different from the sum of their parts. Therapists place no additional value on any part of the person.

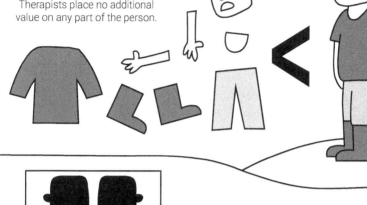

Field Theory
The person as they interact with their environment.
Figure: Notable parts of the individual.
Ground: Unconscious parts of the individual.

Figure-Formation Process
A part of the environment becomes an emphasis for the person.

Oh no, I'm off balance.

Organismic Self-Regulation
A need or interest has knocked the person out of equilibrium. Therapy addresses what clients need to regain equilibrium.

Gestalt Art Therapy

Through Gestalt art therapy, clients are likely to expand their consciousness and awareness by experimenting with art materials. Art making is also a way for individuals to better understand their problems.[59]

In Gestalt art therapy:

Art helps clients experience wholeness, as they can explore themselves as a full person.[60]

One's art product is a "Gestalt" of them in the present moment.[61]

Art making may help clients unstick stuck energy.[62]

Gestalt art therapists may use a technique that involves encouraging clients to speak as if they are each element of their artwork. They may ask clients to describe their artwork by beginning with "I am" or "I feel."[63]

For example, let's take a look at this client who was successful in his career and family but could not shake a sense of hollowness.[64]

Gestalt Art Therapy

Over the following weeks, this client was able to use his artwork to describe his difficult relationship with his mother, who was often harsh, derogatory, and distant. The locker image spoke to his emptiness in trying to please his mother but never earning her acceptance.

As art therapy continued, the client's images shifted from painful themes about his mother to positive relationships with his wife and child. By engaging in creative activities, the client found new meaning in his life.

Cognitive and Postmodern

Cognitive and Postmodern

I'd like to speak about cognitive–behavioral, narrative, and solution–focused approaches.

Key goals for cognitive and postmodern approaches:[65]

Cognitive-Behavioral

Identifying problematic thinking patterns
Replacing or altering damaging behaviors with healthy ones

Narrative

Finding strengths in stories
Externalizing problems and viewing them from unique perspectives

Solution-Focused

Finding what is working and building upon strengths

Cognitive-Behavioral Theory

Albert Ellis and Aaron T. Beck were main contributors to much of the theory underlying cognitive-behavioral therapy. Cognitive-behavioral approaches assume that dysfunction stems from one's perceptions of an experience rather than the experience itself.[66]

Another assumption is that people learn irrational thinking patterns which affect their behaviors. Through cognitive-behavioral therapy, clients work to either alter damaging behaviors or replace destructive behaviors with healthy ones.

One of Aaron Beck's contributions was the "negative cognitive triad," which involves an individual's negative perspectives of the self, the world, and the future.

Cognitive Distortions

Aaron Beck identified several cognitive distortions that affect humans' functioning.[67] Let's look at these from the perspective of a student.

Cognitive Distortions

I got an F on a history test in fifth grade. I couldn't possibly make it through graduate school!

Overgeneralization

Applying the experience of one event to all other events.

I dropped coffee on my pants, I was late to class, and I forgot my laptop. The world is out to get me.

Personalization

Incorrectly correlating external experiences to oneself.

I got a terrible grade!

Surely you mean an **average** grade?

Inexact Labeling

Using language that is out of proportion with the actual event or experience.

If I don't get straight As, I'm a complete failure.

Dichotomous Thinking

Thinking only in either/or scenarios.[68]

Techniques

Clients and therapists work together to establish and work toward realistic goals. Cognitive-behavioral therapists tend to be active, directive, and problem-focused and are likely to utilize effective techniques.[69]

Psychoeducation

Teaching clients about the underlying causes of their problems.

Environmental, genetic, and biological factors contribute to anxiety.

Positive Reinforcement

Presenting a stimulus after desired behavior to strengthen the behavior.

Well done!

Thanks!

I want to continue doing well.

Coping Skills

Encouraging clients to practice healthy ways to handle emotions.

Next time I get mad, I can take some deep breaths.

Changing Self-Talk

Identifying imprecise language and learning to think and speak realistically.

When I make a mistake, I need to stop calling myself an idiot. It's just a mistake!

Humor

Learning to laugh at problematic thinking.

It is funny I got so worked up over that little thing! How silly!

Techniques[70]

Relaxation Techniques

Using breathing, visualization, and muscle relaxation techniques to relieve stress.

I'm doing my best.

Yeah! I'm doing my best, too!

Modeling

Demonstrating positive behaviors.

Try out this journal to record your thoughts and feelings. You can use words, imagery, or both!

Self-Management Principles

Observing and recording one's own behaviors, often through the use of homework (tasks given between sessions to practice skills outside of therapy).

Thanks!

Reality Shaping

Creating imagery to identify and organize dysfunctional patterns.

Cognitive-Behavioral Art Therapy

Cognitive-behavioral art therapy[71] can be particularly beneficial in enhancing decision-making and problem-solving skills. Creating may also benefit clients who are working to enhance focused attention and develop an internal locus of control.

Cognitive-behavioral art therapists may utilize some of the following techniques:

- Using art making to identify coping strategies

- Comparing and contrasting drawings

- Helping individuals visualize and reframe negative events

- Creating visual images of feelings

- Altering negative images to create positive ways of thinking

- Visual journaling as homework to easily recognize patterns

A computer programmer participated in art therapy sessions after severe depression led to their hospitalization. They wanted to understand their emotions and how to express them more safely.[72]

In one session, the art therapist recommended creating two different drawings: one for life before entering the hospital and one for what the client hoped to achieve through outpatient services.

The client's first drawing featured ups and downs, as well as a final "dip" to represent their depression. The second drawing included some grassy hills, and the client explained that the drawing represented their desire to be more stable. They also wanted more warmth, so they added a sun.

Art therapy helped the client become more mindful of their emotions, which led to greater control over their anxiety and depression.

Mindfulness-Based Art Therapy

Mindfulness-based art therapy (MBAT)[73] is a subcategory of cognitive-behavioral art therapy. Mindfulness, rooted in Buddhism, involves placing one's focus on the present moment. The combination of mindfulness and art therapy aims to channel one's "inner witness" to become more aware of their external experiences.

Involving oneself in art making is likely to enhance mindfulness, as a "flow" state often occurs. When an artist is in a flow state, it means that they have fully immersed themselves in the experience through gradual challenges and may lose track of time. Warren stated that flow can help clients understand their true identities and face problems that occur in everyday life.

Along with producing a flow state, the following are a few ways in which art therapy can promote mindfulness:

- Individuals can practice focusing on their moment-to-moment awareness while they experiment with a variety of art materials.

- Clients can visualize and create images of their internal awareness.

- Artists can work to identify emotions and create symbols to represent them.

- Clients can learn art-based relaxation and grounding techniques.

Narrative Therapy

Michael White and David Epston were two of the most significant figures in developing narrative therapy. This approach emphasizes stories that people tell others.[74]

Therapists listen to clients' stories about their problems and search for moments when clients are successful. Therapists find strengths to help clients reauthor their stories through a more positive lens.

Narrative therapy typically features the following goals:

Externalizing the problem.

Separating the individual from their problem.

Separating the guilt from the problem.

Narrative Art Therapy

Art making can be beneficial in externalizing one's problems. Clients can "create their problem" with art materials. The tangible art product makes it easier for the individual to see the problem from a new perspective.[75]

Narrative approaches may be particularly helpful for individuals who have experienced trauma. When a survivor reflects on traumatic memories, it is often difficult to find words to describe the events.

Narrative art therapists may encourage clients to create images of the moments of their traumatic experiences, which can then be rearranged until they are in the correct order. Gradual exposure to the complete and accurate trauma narrative is likely to reduce symptoms associated with trauma. Telling one's story also helps individuals experience a sense of closure so they can begin to move on from the event.

Narrative Art Therapy

The following is a case[76] about a client who participated in art therapy at a domestic violence agency. She was regularly experiencing dissociation, nightmares, flashbacks, and parental stress after surviving emotional, sexual, and physical abuse from her boyfriend. She hoped that she would be able to relieve her symptoms and improve her relationship with her young son.

For the first few sessions, the art therapist focused on psychoeducation about trauma. The client practiced grounding techniques and created a safe-place drawing.

When the client had an understanding of how the process worked and demonstrated tolerance to exploring trauma, the art therapist encouraged her to begin a graphic narrative. Throughout several sessions, the client created moments of her abuse on separate pieces of paper. In one image, the client was shown begging her boyfriend so she could seek medical attention for her son. In another, she drew her abuser holding a gun to his mouth and threatening suicide.

Upon viewing the illustrations, the client could recognize that the incidents were in her past. Toward the end of her treatment, she reported less anxiety and she no longer experienced flashbacks. She felt empowered enough to report the abuse to the police.

Solution-Focused Theory

Insoo Kim Berg and Steve de Shazer are two prominent figures in the development of solution-focused therapy.[77] In this approach, clients are typically encouraged to discuss their experiences and problems, while the therapist guides them toward possible solutions. This approach is typically future-focused and revolves around collaborating to reach the client's goals.

Solution-focused therapists assume that clients know the most about their lives and can therefore come up with their own solutions.

Solution-Focused Principles

The following are some of the dimensions of solution-focused therapy.[78]

Exceptions

Believing there are exceptions
to every problem.

Perspective

Changing perspective on
the problem alters the problem.

Baby Steps

Small changes make a big difference.

Finding Strengths

Looking for what is working.

Future-Focused

Figuring out future possibilities with
little regard to the origin of the problem.

Solution-Focused Art Therapy

In solution-focused art therapy,[79] clients and therapists work together to set realistic goals for the course of therapy. Creating images may be helpful for individuals to see their problems from a unique perspective. After viewing the finished artwork, clients and therapists can work together to identify possible solutions to the problems.

The following techniques of solution-focused therapy can be altered to include visual media:

Exception-Finding Question

The therapist asks about a time when the client was not experiencing their presenting problem.

The Miracle Question

The therapist asks what clients' lives would look like if they woke up the next day without any of their problems.

Contemplative Approaches

Contemplative

Let's take a brief moment to learn about two contemplative approaches: spiritual and focusing-oriented.

Key goals for contemplative approaches:

Spiritual

Developing and maintaining a relationship with a power greater than oneself
Dissolving dualism between body and mind[80]

Focusing-Oriented

Increasing one's "felt sense"[81]

Spiritual Approaches

Therapists who work from contemplative approaches believe that spirituality is a key issue in an individual's overall health. Through therapy, clients can create and maintain a relationship with a greater power than oneself.[82]

Spiritual art therapy utilizes the creative process to help individuals understand and accept their genuine selves. This approach is also helpful in building a pathway between individuals and a higher power. The therapist is a companion along the client's journey.

Spiritual approaches address the following:

Personal Meaning

What does happiness look like for the individual?

Dualism

Breaking down the barrier between one's mind and body.

MIND

BODY

Focusing-Oriented

Rappaport explained that focusing-oriented art therapy was developed from Gendlin's focusing method. Gendlin believed that "focusing" involves concentrating intently on a "felt sense" which occurs when immersing oneself in the present moment. Rappaport noted that creating art is an effective means to access one's "felt sense" and listed the following steps.[83]

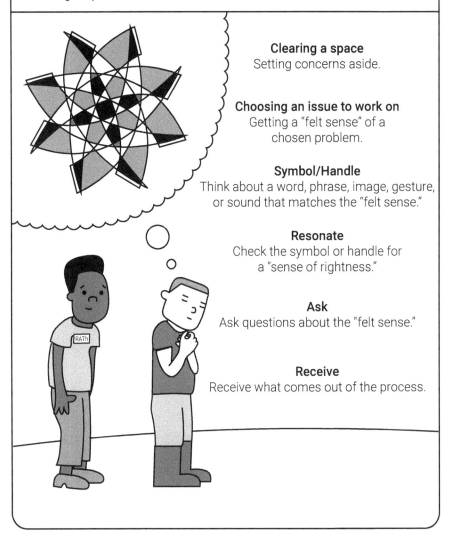

Clearing a space
Setting concerns aside.

Choosing an issue to work on
Getting a "felt sense" of a chosen problem.

Symbol/Handle
Think about a word, phrase, image, gesture, or sound that matches the "felt sense."

Resonate
Check the symbol or handle for a "sense of rightness."

Ask
Ask questions about the "felt sense."

Receive
Receive what comes out of the process.

Systemic Approaches

Systemic approaches look at how individuals' environment and relationships affect them. We'll describe feminist and family approaches first, then we'll touch on group art therapy.

Key goals for systemic approaches:[84]

Feminist

Increasing empowerment
Giving a voice to individuals who have been oppressed

Family

Achieving growth in the entire family system, not just the individual

Group

Social learning
Gaining a sense of belonging

Feminist Theory

Therapists who work from a feminist approach understand that one's social environment affects them. Feminist therapists are advocates of positive social change and typically work to educate others about social justice.[85]

The following are some of the principles of feminist therapy.

Egalitarian Therapeutic Relationship
Therapists decide to utilize appropriate self-disclosure to model openness and normalize experiences. Therapists understand that power dynamics are likely to affect clients.

Privilege
Therapists help clients understand how their identities within society give them privilege.

Oppression
Therapists help clients understand how oppression has affected them. Oppression has a significant impact on mental health.

Empowerment
Therapists help clients to embrace their personal power.

Advocacy
Clients are encouraged to consider themselves as advocates for themselves as well as others.

Interventions

Feminist therapists may use some of these interventions to help clients navigate their problems.[86]

Social Identity Analysis
Understanding how social expectations have molded thoughts and behaviors. Reframing to focus on societal factors that affect clients' problems.

I was always told not to cry or express my feelings as a boy. I guess it's just hard to do that now.

So, as a white man, I have a lot of privilege?

Indeed!

Power Analysis
Gaining information on the power individuals have in society.

Social Action
Encouraging involvement in social action activities to enhance empowerment.

Relabeling
Altering the wording to describe oneself.

Being unemployed does not make me worthless. I am a loving stay-at-home father.

I'm going to start volunteering!

Intersectionality

Talwar explained that individuals have different experiences based on social categories. Identity is complex and involves interconnected aspects of oneself.[87] Intersectionality, a term coined by Kimberlé Crenshaw, is a theory that individuals are affected by all of their social identities.

Intersectionality might look a little like this:

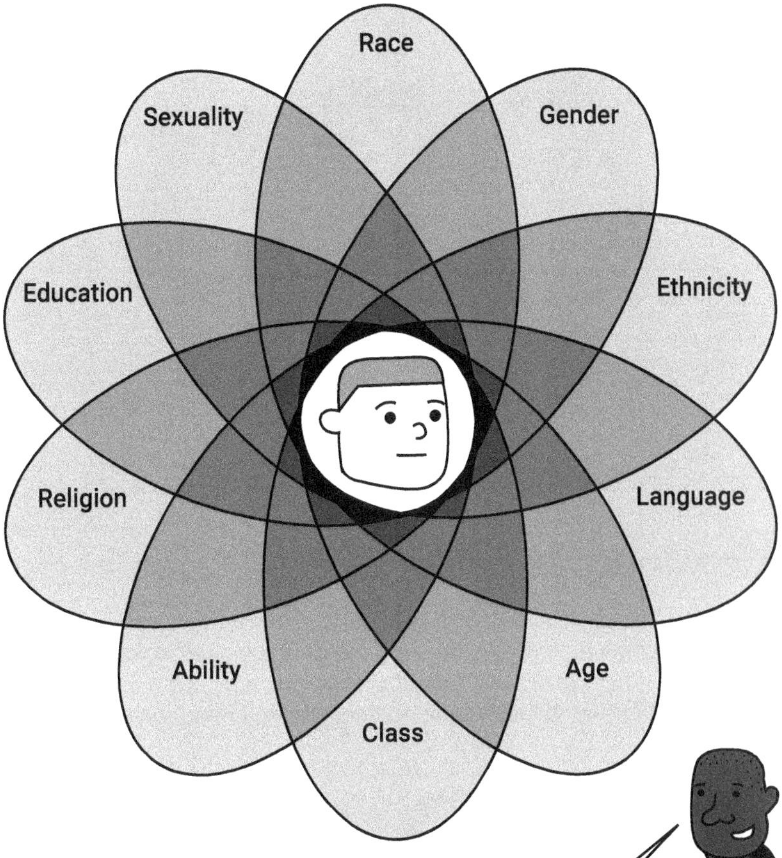

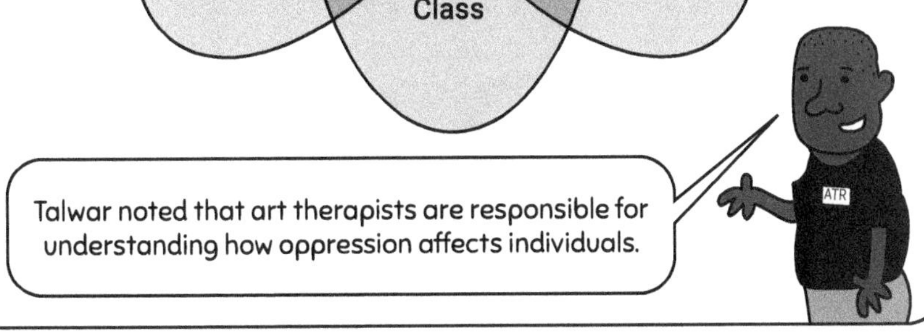

Race
Sexuality
Gender
Education
Ethnicity
Religion
Language
Ability
Age
Class

Talwar noted that art therapists are responsible for understanding how oppression affects individuals.

Feminist Art Therapy

Group art therapy may be particularly helpful for women, as their experiences can be normalized through others' stories. Women can experience validation and determine how internalized messages about their roles in society have affected them.[88]

Contrary to what some may think, feminist therapy approaches are also effective with men. Men can learn about the privileges they experience and can explore how to reimagine masculinity and femininity.

Family Therapy

Murray Bowen and Virginia Satir were prominent figures in the development of family therapy. In this theory, individuals are understood within the context of their family system. The following are assumptions of family therapy.[89]

An individual family member's problematic behaviors may...

1. Serve as a function or purpose for the family
2. Be unintentionally maintained by family processes
3. Be a function of the family's inability to operate productively, especially during developmental transitions
4. Be a symptom of generational dysfunctional patterns

Through family therapy sessions, the therapist emphasizes the need for the entire family system to adjust perspectives and patterns, as well as discover solutions. This means that the "identified patient" is not the focus of therapy.

Genograms

One effective way to gather information about a family is through the use of genograms. They involve mapping out at least three generations of a family, including names, ages, and birthdates.[90]

Amanda
Age 35
1985

Dan
Age 52
1968

Individual family members may look like this.

Most genograms use circles to represent females and squares to represent males. There are lots of symbols to use when constructing a genogram! A quick web search will bring up a variety of symbols to use!

A family system looks more like this:

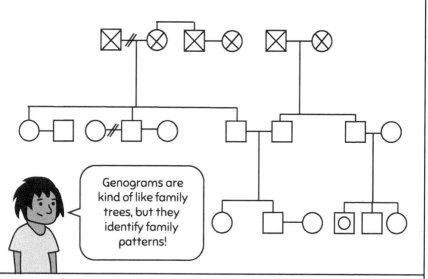

Genograms are kind of like family trees, but they identify family patterns!

Genograms provide a visual way to review family history. Including art making in genograms can be helpful, as members can choose images that define their family, which provides additional insight.[91]

Family Art Therapy

Family art therapy aims to enhance the whole family's ability to communicate with one another and identify strengths and weaknesses in family patterns. The inclusion of art levels the playing field; family members of all ages can participate and have an equal voice in therapy.[92]

Group Art Therapy

Waller outlined the following advantages of art therapy groups.[94]

People typically communicate verbally; art making bypasses well-established verbal defense mechanisms.

You're right, Charles! I didn't realize it when I was drawing, but my artwork is about a need that I haven't been communicating.

Members can be encouraged to experiment with materials as a means of self-expression.

I was hesitant at first, but watching him makes me think I can do this.

I didn't think I'd be good at this, but I'm actually pretty proud of my art!

Reminds me of the "one way" streets downtown.

I think it relates to my future goals.

Makes me think of new beginnings.

Artwork made in groups has symbolic meaning; the meaning may differ between members.

Group Art Therapy

Members may experience free association, and repressed experiences come out through their artwork; the group can process these experiences together.[95]

Evidence of resonance occurs when members produce similar symbols without having seen each other's artwork.[96]

Art products can be used as a means of projection.

Interaction between members may reduce a single member's expectation to have their work interpreted by the facilitator.

Group Art Therapy

In the talk therapy group, I felt like everyone was staring at me. Looking at my art makes me feel less vulnerable.

Compared with traditional talk therapy, art therapy groups may be less intimidating.[97]

The inviting nature of art materials may balance out the seriousness of therapy.

I was really worried about coming to therapy, but I'm having some fun!

Me, too!

The tangible art product serves as a reminder of what occurred in group.

This pendant will remind me to practice self-care.

Art making improves problem-solving and creative thinking skills.

Shoot! I messed up. Wait...I could turn that line into a little bridge!

Examples of Art Therapy Groups

Williams and Tripp described three types of art therapy groups.[98]

Studio/Community-Based

Group members work on their own art, so the facilitator does not provide specific instructions or themes. This approach benefits the community by enhancing creative expression while offering a space for socialization.

> I'd like you to think about your life as a road. What does your road look like?[99]

Theme/Task-Focused

The group facilitator provides a specific directive or theme for all group members to explore. This approach is common for group members with similar problems.

Process-Oriented

The emphasis is placed on group members' interactions with each other, so this type of group could be any combination of directive or nondirective.

Most group facilitators allow time at the end of art making for group members to speak about their artwork.

Considerations

Safety considerations are especially important in group settings, particularly when members have diverse or unknown trauma histories. If one member becomes traumatized, the whole group could be impacted, so directives must be carefully examined before implementing.

The following are additional considerations for art therapy groups.[100]

Is the group long-term or short-term?

How long is each session?

What are the treatment goals for the group?

What are the developmental levels of the individual group members?

It might be too early to introduce a collaborative group project... I should wait until the group members get to know each other more.

Can the group members be safe with the materials I'm providing?

Do I have enough space to store everyone's artwork?

Should I take a directive or nondirective approach?

What is the population like?

If I change direction in the middle of a group, it needs to be for therapeutic gain.

Yalom's Therapeutic Factors

Irvin Yalom identified 11 therapeutic factors that lead to positive changes for members of therapy groups.[101]

All these people can't be wrong! This group is really going to help me!

Instillation of Hope
This is a belief that therapy will help; the group itself instills a sense of hope for members.

That's happened to me, too!

Universality
Other group members have been through the same or similar experiences and can relate to one another. This is difficult to achieve in an individual session.

I've heard it's pretty common for people with our condition to experience flashbacks.

Imparting Information
This is a psychoeducational aspect in which experiences become normalized through learning about myths or tips on handling the problem.

Everyone else in this group has it tough, too. I'm going to make it a point to say something encouraging.

Altruism
Altruism refers to selfless concern for others. Altruistic thoughts and behaviors can break the monotony of cyclical thinking and produce positive feelings.

Yalom's Therapeutic Factors[102]

Corrective Recapitulation of the Primary Family Group

The primary family group, often called the family of origin, is the family that people grow up with. The therapy group is a social microcosm that reflects each member's family of origin. Earlier relationships and experiences are reframed through group processing.

At first, you reminded me of my bossy big brother, Eric. But now that I've gotten to know you, I realize that you both just want to help me.

I didn't like when you interrupted my story.

Development of Socializing Techniques

This involves working on being assertive without being aggressive. This can be the active intent of the therapy group or may be a byproduct of the group setting.

Rich makes eye contact with me when I'm speaking. I should do that, too.

Imitative Behavior

This involves observing others to gain inspiration or learn new social skills. Individuals internalize new behaviors to practice outside of the group.

I was embarrassed to share that with you, but thank you for showing me compassion.

Interpersonal Learning

This factor means learning to connect with others in a meaningful way. Individuals may learn that people are kind, even when sharing experiences based in shame.

Yalom's Therapeutic Factors[103]

Group Cohesiveness

Group cohesiveness is a group's sense of being there for one another. Perception of how much the group helps increases with effective cohesiveness. This does not mean the absence of conflict; it is more about a sense of belonging within the group.

Catharsis

Catharsis is a release of feelings. When catharsis occurs, it is important to pair it with an intellectual understanding.

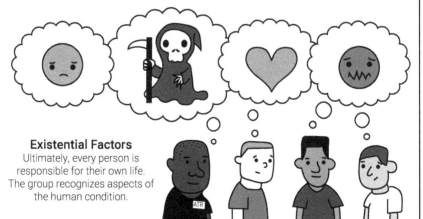

Existential Factors

Ultimately, every person is responsible for their own life. The group recognizes aspects of the human condition.

Group Dynamics

Group art therapists focus on the dynamics between individual group members. Relationship dynamics can be discovered by observing how group members participate.[104] For example...

Who is looking at other people's art?

Who is working independently?

Ooh! Can I go first?

Who offers to share their artwork?

See? Knit one, purl two.

If you get it wrong, oh well. Knit happens!

Who is helping others?

Who is cracking jokes?

The paper's all mine! You can't have any!

Who is struggling to share supplies?

Group Art Therapy Models

This page features three models that art therapists may use in their work with groups.[105] Let's take a closer look.

Analytic

In an analytic model, the agent of change is typically the therapist, whose role is that of a neutral observer. The primary dynamic is the therapist's examination and analysis of transference. Art making is typically nondirective, and the goal is likely to uncover natural resistance in order to enable insight and change.

This model's temporal focus is on personal historical data, both in the far and near past. That's a little different from the other two models!

Interpersonal

The interpersonal model, also known as the interactive model, makes use of the group itself as the agent of change, as the primary dynamic is the actions and behaviors that occur between the members and the therapist. Art therapists are transparent to various degrees and typically use a directive approach to art making. The goal of the group is to create a positive interpersonal experience to transfer to external experiences.

Art-based Group Therapy

The art, including the process and product(s), is the agent of change in an art-based group therapy format. The primary dynamic is communication through art making. The art therapist often creates art along with clients, and the therapist is likely to take a nondirective approach. The goal of an art-based group is to express verbally difficult material, which can lead to catharsis and group acceptance.

The temporal focus for the interpersonal and art-based group therapy models is on the here and now!

Integrative Approaches

From a multicultural perspective, integrative approaches may be ideal, as therapists can find what fits for the client, rather than molding the client to fit their theory.[106]

Types of Integration

The following are variations of integration.[107]

> One of my clients would really benefit from reauthoring their personal story, so I think I will use some narrative techniques.

> Another client seems to struggle with negative self-talk, so cognitive-behavioral therapy techniques would be helpful!

Technical Integration
Identifying and utilizing the best treatment techniques for the specific individual and their problem.

> I consider myself a cognitive-behavioral art therapist, but I am open to other perspectives!

Assimilative Integration
Subscribing to one particular theory but selecting appropriate treatment principles from other theories.

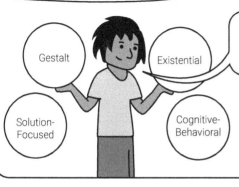

Gestalt

Existential

> Hmm, I see these approaches all emphasize the importance of the "here and now."

Solution-Focused

Cognitive-Behavioral

Common Factors
Looking for the common aspects across theoretical orientations.

Which Approach(es) to Choose?

A beginning art therapist may have a difficult time identifying which approach(es) to choose. Wadeson asserted that individuals should choose approaches depending on the clients' needs.[108]

To illustrate integration and evolution as an art therapist, Wadeson used a metaphor of selecting clothes from different stores. Essentially, it is important that the art therapist combines theories in a way that is effective for the client and the situation.

This person combined theories in a way that is beneficial for the client! Woohoo!

Oh, dear. This is what we call syncretism. This person just used anything that seemed to work.

Corey explained that remaining open and combining approaches based on one's personality is crucial.[109] It is important to consider one's strengths when selecting an approach, so the therapist can be genuine.[110] In other words, don't change yourself to match a theory!

Let's explore some of the

Special Populations

art therapists work with
and how art therapy can
benefit them.

Introduction to Special Populations

So, you know that art therapists work with individuals, groups, families, and communities, but let's take a look at some of the specific populations with which they may work.

The key word here is "some." In the grand scheme of things, art therapists can and do work with just about anyone!

It's true! People of all ages and developmental levels can benefit from art therapy. Art therapy may be particularly helpful for:[1]

People who cannot speak

People who find difficulty putting their thoughts into words

People who have difficulty with communication

People who resist traditional talk therapy

Before we move on to specific populations, let's get one thing straight. Art therapists tend to hear phrases like these a lot.

Pfff... I can't do art therapy! I'm not artistic! I'm not creative! I can't even draw a straight line! I can barely draw stick figures!

Think again!

People do not need to identify as artists to participate in and benefit from art therapy.

Now that that's settled, let's move forward.

Children²

What are this population's needs?

Increasing awareness of impulses

Identifying and expressing feelings

Enhancing healthy creative growth

Fostering self-esteem

Developing an internal sense of order

Enhancing frustration tolerance and enhanced focus

I love sidewalk chalk!

How does art therapy help?

Through artwork, children can explore their fantasies and fears; art making gives them the opportunity to face fears in a safe space.

Children learn patience, cooperation, and sharing in art therapy groups.

The sensory and kinesthetic aspects of art making are helpful in reducing internal tension.

Art making gives the child an opportunity to take control and "be in charge."

Children can learn to master art making and therefore develop self-esteem.

Children learn to direct impulses to acceptable behaviors, such as pounding clay.

Consistency in space, time, and materials helps children develop inner order.

The creative process is empowering, because others can see the finished product.

Children may not have words to express how they feel, so images are more effective.

Child and Adolescent Survivors of Sexual Abuse[3]

What are this population's needs?

Increasing empowerment

Identifying strengths

Regaining trust in others

Developing a new sense of control

Desensitizing traumatic experiences

How does art therapy help?

In art therapy, survivors do not need to use words to describe their experience. This is often an uncomfortable or even impossible topic to discuss verbally.

Art therapy may be less intimidating than talk therapy.

Art therapy spaces are inviting for children and adolescents.

Children and adolescents are more likely to engage in therapy if movement is introduced and encouraged.

Traumatic memories present as visual imagery, so it may be more effective to create art than to speak.

Creating art is empowering and can be used to regain a sense of control.

Survivor of Sexual Abuse: A Vignette

This is the story[4] of a six-year-old female client who had been sexually abused. She participated in art therapy sessions when she was admitted to an acute psychiatric hospital. Her presenting problems were aggression and behavioral issues, including sexually acting out. The art therapist utilized a nondirective approach in their hospital studio.

When the client first entered the studio, she demonstrated impulsivity by immediately collecting art materials. In particular, she gathered large jugs of paint and began pouring them into containers. The art therapist offered assistance, but the client quickly stated that she didn't need any help.

The client mixed all of the paint together and created a muddy mess which seemed symbolic of her mixed feelings toward her abuser. Her descriptions of him were often conflicting. She went back and forth between stating that she loved him and that he was a bad person.

She finger painted with the mixture and explained that she needed to fill the entire piece of paper. She then asked for a box to place her painting in. This pattern of messy painting and containing continued for several sessions. The patient always placed her goopy mess in a box and demanded that the art therapist keep the boxes safe.

Throughout the sessions, the client talked about some of her "messy emotions" surrounding the abuse and, upon discharge, she appeared to have a better understanding of her feelings. When the art therapist offered her boxes to her, the client said they should stay at the hospital. Perhaps this was a way for her to leave her trauma behind.

Autism Spectrum Disorder[5]

This population may experience:

Difficulty with social communication

Repetitive motor movement and speech

Repetitive or fixed behaviors and interests

Atypical sensory processing

What are this population's needs?

Improving fine and gross motor skills

Increasing cooperation and social skills

Boosting abstract thinking skills

I don't usually like slimy stuff, but painting is fun!

How does art therapy help?[6]

Art making is likely to help individuals improve motor coordination and imagination skills.

Art therapists can offer sensory materials and experiences to slowly desensitize individuals who have difficulty with sensory processing.

Group art therapy may help neurodiverse individuals practice social skills. Art making broadens communication.

Visual cues may be helpful in social awareness and emotional learning.

Art therapy may be less frustrating than other approaches, because there is a tangible, visual end goal.

Art therapy can help families find ways to structure home tasks as engaging success experiences!

Attention-Deficit/Hyperactivity Disorder[7]

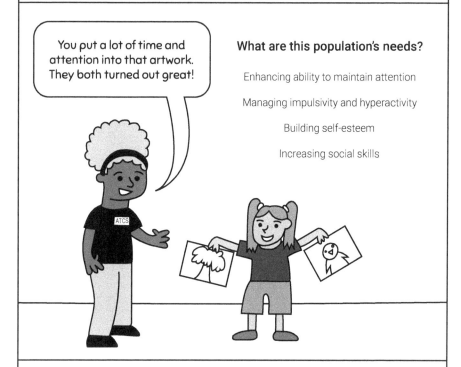

You put a lot of time and attention into that artwork. They both turned out great!

What are this population's needs?

Enhancing ability to maintain attention

Managing impulsivity and hyperactivity

Building self-esteem

Increasing social skills

How does art therapy help?

In art therapy, children can redirect energy "to maintain attention so that it can be applied to listening, learning, and productively using the learned information."[8]

Art making provides a structure to therapy and invites positive experiences.

Individuals can practice strategies for school success.

Art therapy can help families establish boundaries and learn to make home life run more smoothly.

Social, Emotional, and Behavioral Difficulties[9]

PBBTTT!

What are this population's needs?

Enhancing emotional regulation

Reducing or managing overwhelming emotions

Limiting "acting out" behaviors

Decreasing feelings of shame

Improving communication

How does art therapy help?

Using symbolism in artwork creates emotional and psychological distance, which makes it easier to share about personal experiences. This helps individuals decide when and how to be open.

Art therapists can encourage individuals to consider positive aspects of themselves.

Art making can create a sense of mastery to make individuals feel good at something.

Art therapists can facilitate cathartic and kinesthetic activities to improve emotional regulation.

Art therapy provides positive experiences with an adult, which is particularly beneficial to a population who may have few positive encounters with adults.

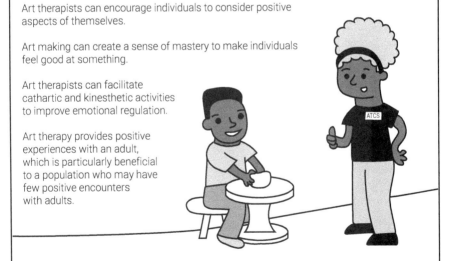

Learning Disabilities[10]

This population is at increased risk for:

Unemployment and social isolation

Limited internal resources to manage emotions

Difficulties with verbal communication

What are this population's needs?

Understanding and expressing complex emotions

Boosting empowerment and autonomy

Increasing social interaction

Feeling safe and contained

sigh

How does art therapy help?

Art provides personalized communication for individuals who are nonverbal or have difficulty with verbal communication.

The art product is an avenue to make clients' voices heard.

Art making enhances individuals' ability to recognize their own thoughts and feelings.

An art therapy group offers an opportunity for individuals to gain confidence while practicing social skills. A judgment-free group encourages a sense of safety and belonging for its members.

Individual with a Learning Disability: A Vignette

The following case[11] is about a young individual who was diagnosed with a learning disability and attention-deficit hyperactivity disorder, which affected her ability to verbally communicate. Due to anxiety about saying things wrong, she had difficulty making friends in her peer group.

In art therapy sessions, she presented as shy and reserved but appeared excited when she looked at the art materials.
For several sessions, the art therapist and
the client made art separately and silently.

After multiple sessions, the art therapist suggested a joint activity. They could continue to work quietly, but they worked together on the same piece of paper. In this way, they could communicate nonverbally and develop a stronger therapeutic relationship. The art therapist mirrored the client's process, which often involved emotional expression.

The silence was important, because the client's communication difficulties were not as obvious in silence. Art therapy offered the client practice in communicating through artwork and having positive experiences with another person. Throughout the sessions, the client built confidence and courage; the client began speaking more regularly in front of her peers.

Adolescents[12]

This population may experience:

Disagreement with authority and/or societal values

Strains in relationships with peers

Withdrawal from family

Negative feelings of being misunderstood or left out

What are this population's needs?

Gaining a sense of control

Affirming a sense of identity

Exploring sexuality and body image

Reducing "acting out" behaviors

How does art therapy help?

Individuals can explore connection and attachment through personal art making.

Art making is effective in safely expressing negative emotions. The art creates a distance between the individual and the emotion.

Personal art expression can encourage individuals to achieve a sense of identity.

The art is under individuals' control; their choices create the final product.

Individuals may use metaphor in their artwork, which creates an indirect way to discuss their problems.

LGBTQIA+ Community[13]

This population is at increased risk for:

Depression and anxiety

Suicide

Discrimination

Bullying and harassment

Emotional disturbances

Drug and alcohol dependency

What are this population's needs?

Reducing feelings of confusion or isolation

Exploring sexual orientation and/or gender identity

Coping with stigma and discrimination

Improving self-esteem and emotional safety

How does art therapy help?

Art therapists can encourage individuals to safely explore their identities related to societal norms.

Art therapists help individuals identify stigma and hatred surrounding their identities. Group work may be particularly helpful for individuals to share experiences with others.

Art therapy can improve emotional safety.

Eating Disorders[14]

This population may experience:

A need for control

A distorted sense of self

Issues with body image

Obsessive thoughts about food

Arguments with others about food and dieting

Increased anxiety

What are this population's needs?

Improving body image and self-acceptance

Improving problem-solving skills

How does art therapy help?

Through art making, clients can take an active role in their own recovery and treatment.

Art therapy can help individuals abandon the idea that their appearance is the most important aspect of their lives.

The freedom to create may help individuals learn how to be their authentic selves.

Visually representing and therefore externalizing the disorder may help individuals view the problem more objectively.

Art therapy may help individuals reintroduce positive qualities to themselves.

Art therapy may also benefit clients by helping them reconnect with their own voices, as opposed to focusing on what others want them to be.

Art making can reduce anxiety.

Addictions/Substance Abuse[15]

What are this population's needs?

Addressing and reducing shame associated with addiction

Reducing isolation

Reducing the need for control

Increasing safe behaviors

How does art therapy help?

Certain art experiences can facilitate feelings of safety and decrease the perceived need for self-control.

Individuals can receive affirmations from others in group art therapy. A supportive environment can help individuals make connections.

Art therapy helps individuals let go of damaging messages from society.

In art therapy, individuals can learn to break damaging self-made rules, such as perfectionism or fear of change.

Art making can help individuals communicate and express repressed emotions.

Art therapy can lead to overcoming denial, a primary goal in addiction treatment.

Depression[16]

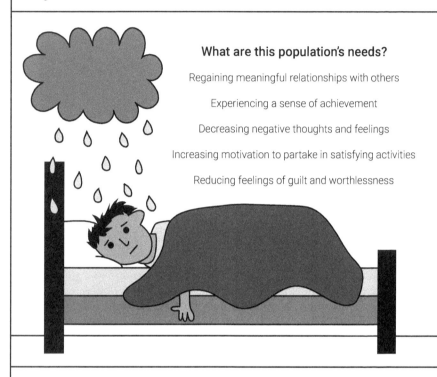

What are this population's needs?

Regaining meaningful relationships with others

Experiencing a sense of achievement

Decreasing negative thoughts and feelings

Increasing motivation to partake in satisfying activities

Reducing feelings of guilt and worthlessness

How does art therapy help?

Group work may be helpful in reducing social withdrawal associated with depression.

Art making enhances individuals' creativity and motivation.

Art therapy can help individuals effectively accept and express emotions and increase their awareness of emotions.

Art therapy presents an opportunity for positive changes in life.

Individuals can learn to accept what does and does not work, both in art making and in real-life situations.

Positive experiences in art therapy can interrupt negative thoughts.

Art making can add meaning to one's life.

Medical Settings[17]

What are this population's needs?

Regaining control and autonomy

Rebuilding a sense of hope and self-esteem

Confronting mortality and finding meaning in life

Coping with the illness, injury, or disease process

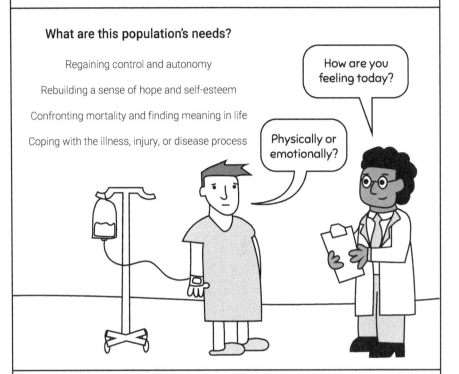

How does art therapy help?

Art making gives medical patients a sense of control and autonomy.

Inviting materials, in the midst of treatments involving pills or needles, may provide comfort.

Art therapy helps individuals discover their strengths and rebuild human connection.

The process of art making can help people cope with pain or discomfort.

Individuals can communicate more effectively with hospital staff by using visuals.

Individuals become active participants in treatment through art making.

When considering the transition after treatment, Councill suggested encouraging individuals to make scrapbooks so they can reconnect with others.

Personality Disorders[18]

What are this population's needs?

Being able to experience a
stable sense of self

Regulating, understanding,
and expressing emotions

Developing problem-solving skills

How does art therapy help?

Art therapy can help individuals improve their sensory perception,
emotional regulation, and insight.

Individuals can learn to
experience a positive
sense of self.

Art making may help individuals
express their emotions.

Borderline Personality Disorder: A Vignette

This case[19] follows a client who participated in art therapy groups in a rehabilitation center. All group members were women who were diagnosed with borderline personality disorder. The client had a history of emotional and physical abuse, and she regularly struggled with self-harm.

Throughout several sessions, the art therapist noticed that most of the client's artwork featured idyllic characters that had been marred in some way. For example, in one session, the client created an image of an angel.

The angel, along with the client's series of similar characters, may have symbolized the client herself. The dirt on the wings may have represented the abuse she had survived.

The client received support from the group and was able to gain insight through her imagery. The art therapy studio became a safe space for her to sublimate her urges to self-harm by engaging in drawing and painting.

Schizophrenia/Psychosis[20]

What are this population's needs?

Reducing internal and social stigma surrounding the illness

Reducing hopelessness and self-doubt

Strengthening a sense of self

Regaining social and vocational roles

Gaining a sense of control as the ability to distinguish between external and internal experiences decreases

How does art therapy help?

Individuals may add an identity as an artist, instead of thinking of themselves as solely a "person with mental illness."

Connection with another person may break up internal cycles.

Art may help individuals externalize their inner reality so the therapist can better understand what they are experiencing.

Art therapists provide a space for individuals to discuss unusual experiences without fear of judgment.

This is kind of what my mind looks like.

Grief and Loss

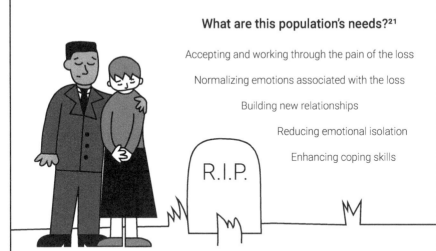

What are this population's needs?[21]

Accepting and working through the pain of the loss

Normalizing emotions associated with the loss

Building new relationships

Reducing emotional isolation

Enhancing coping skills

How does art therapy help?[22]

Individuals can recreate themselves by expressing and transforming their feelings.

Art making can preserve positive memories of the deceased loved one.

Creating artwork in memory of a deceased loved one may help them accept their loss.

Through art therapy support groups, members can connect with one another and share stories, which can promote healing and hope.

Uncle Larry loved playing with Scruffy!

Larry with Kaitlyn and Trish at the zoo.

Survivors of Domestic Violence and/or Abuse[23]

This population may have experienced:

Physical and/or sexual assault

Manipulation and isolation

Betrayal and humiliation

What are this population's needs?

Gaining positive relationships and social support

Building agency and resistance

Adjusting to home and family changes

Restoring a sense of identity

Effective safety planning

How does art therapy help?

Discussing abuse is often difficult or even impossible. Art making may provide a less intimidating way for survivors to tell their stories.

Art therapy renews individuals' sense of empowerment by giving them a voice.

Art therapy may provide positive experiences between mothers and children.

Art therapy, paired with psychoeducation, may be effective in preventing future instances of violence and/or abuse.

Art therapists can educate clients about the cycle of violence.

Clients can learn to identify triggers that cause strong emotions.

Homelessness[24]

What are this population's needs?

Building resilience, coping with stress, and setting goals

Gaining self-esteem, self-determination, and reconnecting with strengths

Establishing and maintaining internal and external support systems

How does art therapy help?

Art therapists provide a safe space to distract individuals from stressful situations.

By taking part in creative activities, individuals practice resiliency and problem-solving.

Individuals may begin to see art as a constant in their lives.

Individuals can begin building a support system within the artist community.

Practicing and mastering art may enhance an individual's sense of identity as an artist.

Individuals may be able to sell artwork to support financial needs.

Combat Veterans[25]

What are this population's needs?

Relieving guilt

Alleviating symptoms of trauma
due to combat

Reducing stigma surrounding mental disorders

Easing the transition back to civilian life

Handling painful emotions

Reconnecting with others

How does art therapy help?

Art making provides distance to safely reexperience the events that may otherwise be difficult to discuss. Visual narratives may be effective in addressing trauma.

Art therapy may help individuals identify their sources of stress and provide a way to boost individuals' ability to manage their stress.

Group art therapy may be particularly effective in helping veterans connect with others who have had similar experiences.

Art making provides a way for veterans to contain powerful emotions and externalize their fears through use of symbols and metaphors.

Art therapy may help individuals break down traditional views of masculinity, which may be a barrier in seeking mental health services.

Combat Veteran: A Vignette

The following case[26] is about a client who had previously served 15 years in the army. His presenting problems included anxiety, social isolation, night terrors, and an exaggerated startle response. He was a member of a 12-session art therapy group specifically for veterans.

In the first session, he created a window.

I guess I feel like a window is opening for me. I'm hopeful about this group being able to help me.

In his second image, he painted a bowl and a can of beans. He had drawn a spoon to transfer the beans from the can to the bowl, though the beans were spilling.

I've been opening up a lot in this group, and I feel like it's been a spoonful at a time. It feels better for me this way, instead of talking about all the traumatic things I've been through right away.

In one of the final sessions, he painted tear drops being absorbed by a poppy.

This group has been a safe space to talk about really tough stuff.

Throughout the art therapy group, the client developed an ability to safely express his difficult emotions by using symbolic imagery. The group provided a container for him to discuss his traumatic experiences, which he had previously been unable to do.

Older Adults[27]

This population may experience:

Depression or grief

Physical limitations or illness

Isolation

Cognitive deficits

Loss of identity

What are this population's needs?

Increasing socialization

Improving cognitive functioning

Regaining a sense of control

Regulating emotions

Practicing self-expression

How does art therapy help?

Certain art activities can help clients improve their cognitive functioning by recalling memories and using problem-solving skills.

Art can be helpful in regulating emotions, either through calming processes or by expressing feelings.

Art therapy provides social interaction, whether with the art therapist or in a group therapy setting.

Art therapy involves and improves sensorimotor activity.

Making art increases empowerment through choice.

Dementia[28]

This population may experience:

Memory impairment

Limited verbal communication

An altered view of reality

Agitation and restlessness

What are this population's needs?

Soothing internal stimuli

Slowing cognitive decline

Improving quality of life

How does art therapy help?

Art therapists can provide a safe environment for individuals to actively create.

Art making can be soothing for individuals experiencing inner turmoil.

Individuals experiencing difficulty with verbal communication can speak through artwork.

Art making makes use of complex cognitive processes and provides stimulation.

Disaster Responses[29]

This population may experience:

Being a witness to death, injury, and destruction

Psychological stress from triggers

Intrusive thoughts about the event

Hypervigilance

Hypersensitivity

What are this population's needs?

Relieving survivor's guilt

Rediscovering life's meaning

Instilling future hope

Learning to cope with loss and trauma

Identifying and managing responses to triggers

How does art therapy help?

Debriefing after a disaster enhances survivors' ability to cope with grief and trauma.

Clients can express and gain control over difficult feelings, such as fear, guilt, and dread.

A nonverbal approach to therapy provides distance from painful memories. Clients can share their experiences when they are ready.

Art therapists may suggest visual journals so clients can work when needed.

Many survivors talk about their experiences until they no longer can; art therapy provides the silence and active but nonverbal processing that survivors may need.

Art therapy is flexible, as individuals of all ages and backgrounds can participate.

Group art therapy may restore a sense of unity.

Disaster Response: A Vignette

This vignette[30] follows a group of children who experienced trauma due to a destructive tsunami. They met for several hour-long art therapy sessions.

In the first group, the art therapist encouraged participants to draw or paint something important in their lives. Many of the children illustrated images of the ocean, because their parents were fishermen and needed the water to survive. After the tsunami, the children were fearful of the ocean, so the artwork contained their conflicting emotions.

In the next session, the art therapist suggested drawing "the day you will never forget."[31] This directive gave the children control over what to draw. While some children created images of the tsunami, others were not ready to explore their trauma and drew special events.

I drew my birthday cake!

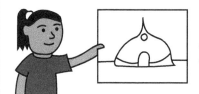

In the third week, the art therapist invited the children to draw somewhere they felt safe. Many of the images were temples, where the tsunami survivors were offered support.

In the fourth session, the children created their hopes for the future. Many of the children drew fairies, which may have symbolized hope and beauty.

Throughout the sessions, the children were able to share the trauma that they could not yet verbalize, which led to gradual healing of collective grief.

Displacement[32]

What are this population's needs?

Rebuilding a sense of support and security

Giving individuals a voice

Learning to regain trust

Exploring one's identity

Restoring normalcy

How does art therapy help?

Art therapy provides individuals a safe space to explore their identities, which can empower them to discover a new sense of self.

Art therapy gives individuals control over their stories and provides opportunities to share their narratives with others.

Engaging in art making may provide a sense of normalcy.

Creating a project that depicts the land they left may help clients establish a connection with that community.

Introduction to Techniques and Directives

Art therapists have a variety of tools to utilize, but it is important not to choose haphazardly. The effective art therapist selects interventions based on the goals their clients are working toward.[1]

Beginning art therapists may initially look for pre-planned directives to use, but after developing their skills, they are likely to come up with their own interventions. Art therapists may also use a more nondirective approach and encourage the client to lead the way.

Rubin noted that art therapists consider three elements when deciding on an intervention.

Media

Remember the Expressive Therapies Continuum? That sure comes in handy when deciding on media. The art therapist also needs to consider the safety of supplies.

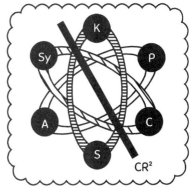

I'm working with a homogeneous group, so I think a theme would be beneficial!

I'll have them warm up for a few minutes with their non-dominant hand.

Theme

The art therapist can decide whether or not a theme would be helpful for their client(s).

Manner of Working

Does the art therapist encourage clients to work in silence, or can they chat while they're working? How long do they work on any given image? What method(s) will the clients use to complete their artwork?

Nondirective vs. Directive

Nondirective and directive approaches benefit clients at different stages in therapy. The approach a therapist chooses depends on the individual and their needs.[3]

Individuals who have not recently participated in art making may enjoy the opportunity to experiment with a variety of materials. These clients may therefore benefit from a nondirective approach.

I'm glad I didn't have to make anything specific... it's been a while since I've used these materials!

I'm glad I was given the directive, "draw yourself as an animal." It gave me a starting place, and I enjoyed thinking of myself this way!

On the other hand, providing a specific directive may help clients feel at ease if they typically require structure and direction.[4]

As always, remember that specific approaches are best utilized by tailoring them to clients' unique needs.

Warm-Ups

Warm-ups typically only last a few minutes, but they can be extremely beneficial. These exercises are fairly simple, and they help clients become familiar with specific art materials and the creative process.[5]

Art therapy warm-ups are just like jumping jacks for creativity!

I guess you can put it that way...

Liebmann offered several ideas for warm-ups to use with clients:[6]

Draw, paint, or sculpt with your eyes closed.

Begin by drawing a circle. Then turn the circle into something.
For example, is it a basketball? Is it a wheel on a car? Is it an aerial view of a witch's cauldron? Is it a pizza? How about a turtle shell?

Create patterns with lines and shapes.

Take a line "for a walk." What direction is the line heading? Is it walking in zigzags, in curves, or in scribbles?

These are just a few examples of the many warm-ups art therapists may suggest to get clients invested in the art-making process.

Scribbling and Squiggling

Florence Cane developed the scribble technique,[7] in which clients engaged in spontaneous expression by scribbling and then finding images in the scribbles. This technique is especially valuable in psychoanalytic approaches, as this is another form of free association.[8]

You may have heard that Margaret Naumburg created the scribble technique. She did use scribbling in art therapy, but original credit is due to her sister, Florence Cane!

D.W. Winnicott developed "the squiggle game," which began with the therapist creating a squiggle; the client would then find images in the squiggle. Then the client created a squiggle for the therapist. This helped build rapport between therapist and client.[9]

Another activity that involves scribbling is the "scribble chase." In this technique, one person begins a scribble and another person follows their line with a different color. Much like the previous two activities, the individuals are then asked to find images in the scribbles and add details to bring out the images they see.[10]

Kramer's Third Hand

Edith Kramer described her concept of the "third hand" as a technique for therapists to help individuals with the creative process without intruding on their ideas or preferences.

Kramer explained that, when using the third hand, it is important for an art therapist to...

- Work with the client on a common task

- Set aside their personal style so they do not change the art's meaning

- "Rescue" images that clients may want to destroy or abandon. The therapist can help fix mistakes through problem-solving

- Stay on the same developmental level as the client[11]

Mandalas

Mandala is the Sanskrit word for "circle" which, in a sense, means "whole." Mandalas are powerful symbols in many Eastern cultures. Carl Jung was thought to have introduced mandalas to Western society. In a Jungian approach, they are considered representative of the human psyche and are associated particularly with spiritual wholeness.[12]

Mandalas are often created by starting with a circle format. From there, clients can fill the circle with patterns and colors by using art materials.

Making mandalas is often beneficial for clients who are working on relaxation techniques, emotional expression, meditation, and self-awareness.

Using Color

Art therapists may encourage clients to use color to express their emotions. There are several common associations between colors and feelings, but clients are likely to be encouraged to identify what colors personally mean to them. For example, while "red" may seem like an "angry" color to many, perhaps an individual thinks red should be reserved for "excited" feelings.[13]

Art therapists may use a fairly nondirective approach by asking clients to use color to express the emotion they're currently experiencing or explore a variety of color associations.[14]

While correlating color and feelings is a common approach, Liebmann suggested alternative ways to use color. For example:

- Filling paper with color as quickly as possible

- Using color to represent other concepts, such as personality traits, family members, or seasons

- Representing opposites by using colors that clients like and dislike[15]

Feeling Map

One specific directive to encourage use of color was utilized by John Goff Jones. Jones worked with survivors of the 1993 bombing in Oklahoma City; he wrote about his work in helping individuals record and understand their emotions. One of his interventions was a "feeling map."[16]

Jones suggested the following instructions for the feeling map:

"Use a different color to represent the following feelings: joy, fear, sadness, love of self, love of others, and anger. Let the strength and nature of the feeling inside you determine the size, shape, and color of the expressed feeling. Please do not use stick figures or happy face characters to represent your feelings. Don't worry about the size, shape, etc., just let the feeling flow from within you."[17]

Jones found this directive helpful in determining clients' progress throughout treatment. The task provided a visual record for the client and the art therapist to review.

Containers

Containers, such as boxes, bags, and jars, are symbolic of protection or safe keeping. Individuals can make containers their own by painting, drawing, or collaging on them. The following are a few ways in which containers may be used as interventions.

Worry Box[18]
Clients write down anxious thoughts and place them inside a container of their own design. This is a tangible way to let go of worry.

Safe Container[19]
Individuals can write things that they are not yet comfortable discussing in therapy and place them in a box. The container keeps thoughts safe until clients are ready to talk about them.

Care Package[20]
Clients fill a box or bag with comforting items for when they aren't feeling well.

Positive Affirmations[21]
Individuals embellish a box in which they can hold on to positive affirmations.

ALL MY WORRIES

I don't need to repress my worry, but sometimes it's helpful to have it contained!

Self-Portraits

Self-portraits can be used when working toward a variety of therapeutic goals. The following are a few variations of self-portraits.

Emotional Expression

Using color to represent the emotions that the client is feeling.[22]

I used mostly greys and blues, because I've been feeling kind of down lately.

Dual Portraits

Representing two aspects in the same portrait or creating two different portraits.[23]

Current self
vs.
Future self

How you feel
vs.
How you present yourself

Perceived self
vs.
Ideal self

How you see yourself
vs.
How others see you

Family Portraits[24]

Creating family portraits is beneficial for exploring family dynamics, as well as how the family system affects each individual member.

Buchalter wrote about constructing figurines to represent different family members while encouraging clients to create at least two figures. The figurines could then be placed on paper and clients could draw an environment around them.[25]

Of course, family portraits can also be created with a variety of drawing, painting, and three-dimensional materials.

After creating family portraits, discussion surrounds which family members were represented and reasons they were chosen. Therapist and client can also discuss the figures' sizes and where they are placed in the artwork.

Collages

When considering media choices, collage may be one of the least threatening. Collage does not require drawing, painting, or sculpting, which may intimidate clients who have not produced art in a long time. Through the process of selecting and pasting materials and images, collage can enhance decision-making skills and provide a means of nonverbal communication.[26]

Buchalter listed the following ideas for collage:[27]

- Creating collages for one's real home and their dream home. Clients can discuss their current home life and ways to improve their living situation.

- Making a collage on the theme of "laughter" to reconnect individuals to positive emotions.

- Using magazines to find words and phrases that clients have wanted to say out loud but haven't been willing or able to yet.

- Drawing an abstract design and then cutting it into pieces. Clients can rearrange the pieces into a collage to promote problem-solving skills.

I'm a fan of torn paper collage! I love the process of ripping paper, and I like the texture it produces, too!

Shrinky Dinks®

Shrinky Dinks® are sheets of plastic that shrink when they are heated. Individuals can color the plastic with markers or colored pencils and cut around their image, then watch as their design gets smaller in an oven or toaster oven.

Wolf Bordonaro, Blake, Corrington, Fanders, and Morley wrote about intervention ideas that utilize Shrinky Dinks®:[28]

- Designing charms for medical bracelets to make them more appealing for patients to wear. The personalized charms could serve as reminders of regular practices to manage or improve their health

- Using images to represent emotional conflicts and then literally "shrinking" those conflicts to a manageable size

- Creating tiny images clients keep with them as reminders of hopes, goals, insight, and progress

- Drawing a wild animal and exploring characteristics of the animal. The discussion could lead to how the animal and its traits serve as metaphors for how we respond to one another

Schreiner and Wolf Bordonaro wrote about their use of Shrinky Dinks® with nursing students.[29] The students created metaphors for personal or professional insight to carry into their careers; many students designed symbols of growth, guidance, and strength.

Digital Media and Technology

According to Orr, digital media "creates and allows for manipulation of an image, sound, movement, or words through its underlying byte system."[30] The implementation of digital media and technology in art therapy sessions is becoming increasingly popular.[31]

Digital media can simulate traditional art materials. For example:[32]

Drawing and Painting

Many programs on a computer or tablet feature a digital canvas and a variety of drawing and painting tools.

I prefer digital collage, because my hands don't get messy. Plus, there's an undo button!

Collage

Some digital applications feature preset packages of images. Clients can select, move, and manipulate collage imagery by using a mouse or touch screen.

Photography

Clients can take photos with digital cameras and upload their images into a photo editing program. From there, individuals can manipulate their images or create digital photo albums.

Digital Media and Technology

While digital media can mimic traditional materials, some creative outcomes would be difficult or impossible to achieve without technology. Free and low-cost apps are available, which makes this media accessible.

Animation

Animation is the process of making still images appear to move. Two-dimensional and three-dimensional computer animation, as well as stop-motion animation, are enticing to many clients and may improve their engagement in treatment.[33]

Video and Filmmaking

Clients can use digital cameras and video editing software to create films. Filmmaking requires a series of steps, including planning, filming, shooting, editing, and producing. Johnson believed this medium enhances self-reflection through personal storytelling.[34]

Video Games

Brown and Garner pointed out that video games can be a form of artistic expression. They focused on games that had world building and avatar creation features. In world-building games, clients can create their own personal world. Avatar creation involves selecting and manipulating features to create playable characters.[35]

Another way technology has entered art therapy practice is through telehealth. Telehealth makes it possible for therapists and clients to meet with each other from separate physical locations through the use of secure, synchronous meeting platforms.[36]

Tee-Shirt Art

Tee-shirts are wearable art. They can be embellished with fabric paint, fabric markers, permanent markers, and/or acrylic paint.

Wolf Bordonaro described the therapeutic benefits of tee-shirt design.[37] She educated clients on the history of tee-shirts, including their use to show support for a cause. For example, in the 1960s, tie-dye was worn to express creative departure from social norms.

From there, Wolf Bordonaro invited clients to identify what was important to them and what causes they would like to support. Clients were encouraged to plan out their design by considering which values to include on their shirt, as well as what imagery and symbols could represent the concepts.

The author provided some helpful tips:

- Use an embroidery hoop to provide a mandala shape to work within.

- Place cardboard in the middle of the tee-shirt to avoid the pigment from going through to both sides.

- Use a pencil to sketch the design first.

- Send written directions for setting pigments home with the client.

Wolf Bordonaro described alternative uses for tee-shirt art:

- Tie-dyeing multiple shirts to be worn by a group, thus creating a sense of community and belonging

- Encouraging school staff members or medical teams to embellish undershirts with symbols of strength to wear as "armor"

- Inviting a group to create a collaborative design which all members replicate on their shirts

Journals

Visual journals work well as homework between sessions. Art therapists may encourage clients to share what they produced in their journal outside of the session, though clients ultimately have control over whether they share or not.

Journals may encourage individuals to develop their own style of artwork or identify new ways to express themselves. Clients can freely experiment between sessions by filling their journal with writing, imagery, or a combination of the two.[38]

Mims used visual journaling with veterans and saw improvement in clients' self-knowledge, confidence, and self-awareness.[39] Jones used a therapeutic journaling technique with survivors of a disaster to help record their progress in therapy.[40]

A standard sketchbook can be used as a visual journal. Clients date the pages and are encouraged to create artwork on each page.

No sketchbook? No problem! Loose-leaf paper and a binder can make for an excellent starter sketchbook.

Comic Strips and Cartoons

Drawing cartoons or comic strips puts clients in charge of writing and illustrating stories of their lives. This approach is also helpful for the art therapist to learn more about the client's world.

Liebmann described a simple directive of drawing cartoons to tell a story.[41]

Drew suggested beginning a group by laying out several comics and asking clients what they like about them. This may help them develop their own illustration or writing style. Another warm-up involves coming up with themes and inviting clients to consider a personal story related to the topic.[42]

Drew encouraged offering sticky notes to illustrate different parts of a scene. That way, clients can easily rearrange the scenes if needed.

Collaboration comics promote social skills and teamwork. Drew suggested giving one person a piece of paper and a minute to draw an image. The client then passes the paper to the person next to them to add another image. This continues until every group member has made an addition. After the group completes the illustration, they can work together to come up with a story and title for their narrative.

Comics often use humor, which can help individuals safely release negative emotions and provide insight.[43]

Puppets and Masks

Puppet making is a safe way for individuals to project their thoughts and feelings onto something else.

Using a puppet for role-playing provides distance for individuals to discuss difficult emotions or situations.[44]

Masks serve as an excellent metaphor for the various aspects of people's personalities or the different roles they play in their lives. Art therapists may encourage clients to design the inside and outside of the mask to represent two sides:[45]

How you see yourself vs. how others see you
Ideal self vs. unacceptable self
Public self vs. private self

Collaborative Artwork

When working with groups or families, collaborative artwork can promote socialization and togetherness, as well as cooperation and problem-solving. The following are a few examples of art therapy directives that encourage at least two people to work on one image.

Dyad Drawings

Two people drawing together on the same piece of paper. This technique helps individuals practice nonverbal communication.[46]

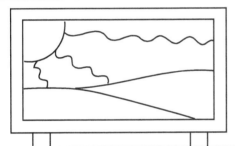

Collaborative Murals

Groups work together to identify a theme for the mural, as well as responsibilities for each member. This can be particularly helpful in enhancing decision-making and problem-solving skills.[47]

One-at-a-Time Group Drawing

One client begins a drawing while the others watch. The client then passes the paper to the next person until everyone has had a turn.[48]

Body Outlines and Body Tracing

Luzzatto, Sereno, and Capps discussed the use of body outlines with cancer patients. They offered a gender-neutral body outline and encouraged clients to fill the image with colors and forms. Clients were able to communicate their current state through their artwork.[49]

Hinz worked with individuals with eating disorders. She taped a piece of butcher paper to the wall and encouraged clients to estimate what their body outline looked like. She then invited clients to draw their body outline. When they completed the drawing, the therapist traced the client's true outline with a different color. Hinz noted that patients typically overestimate their body size, so this activity was helpful in identifying difficulties in perception.[50]

Martin suggested using body tracing with children with autism. Children learned how to work as a team when they took turns tracing each other's outline. This activity enhanced body awareness, body control, and patience.[51]

Bridge Drawings

Hays and Lyons developed and researched the bridge drawing as a projective assessment as well as a therapeutic intervention for individuals in substance abuse treatment.[52]

They used the following script:

"Draw a picture of a bridge going from some place to some place." When the participants were finished, they added, "Indicate with an arrow the direction of travel. Place a dot to indicate where you are in the picture." Participants were invited to write about their drawings, as well.

The authors noted the following variables in the drawings:

Directionality: The left side of the paper was typically viewed as the past, whereas the right was perceived as the future.

Placement of self in the picture: How far have they traveled? Are they close to meeting a goal?

Places drawn on either side of the bridge: How are they different or similar, and what does this indicate based on the directionality of past and future?

Solidarity of the bridge attachments: Does the bridge have a firm foundation?

Emphasis by elaboration: Is there a psychological meaning to an area that is overworked?

Bridge construction: Is the bridge sturdy? What is the bridge made out of?

Type of bridge: Is it a traffic bridge, rope bridge, or garden bridge?

Matter drawn under the bridge: Is anything under the bridge, and if so, is it threatening?

Vantage point of the viewer: Is the perspective from eye level, from above, from below, or a bird's eye view?

Axis of the paper: Is the paper vertical or horizontal?

Consistency of Gestalt: Is the imagery mostly harmonious or incongruous?

Written associations to the drawing: Did they mention what the bridge crossed over? Perhaps they explained what was on either side of the bridge?

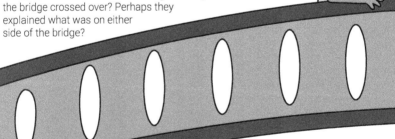

Bridge Drawings

Bridge drawings can be helpful as therapeutic interventions, as they offer the opportunity to make connections and improve problem-solving. Many of the variables previously noted could help clients gain insight and open communication in the therapeutic relationship. For example:[53]

- Directionality may suggest if individuals desire regression or progress.
- The vantage point may provide information on one's communication style.
- The construction of the bridge can bring insight on the individual's commitment to their goal(s). Individuals can then decide how to strengthen their bridge, if needed.
- In a group setting, members can challenge each other's placement of self.

Holt and Kaiser wrote about their recovery bridge directive, in which they gave the following prompt: "Complete a bridge depicting where you have been, where you are now, and where you want to be in relation to your recovery."[54]

Schmanke used the bridge drawing with clients in substance abuse treatment. She altered the directive to: "Draw a picture that has a bridge and a person in it. You can add anything else you want."[55] Schmanke found value in assessing the drawing of the person as well as in allowing the prompt to remain ambiguous until verbal processing took place. She elaborated on several variables, including:[56]

Depiction of person: The location of the person in the drawing, their engagement with the environment, and emotional aspect are possible unconscious projective indicators or intentional "faking good" depictions.

Paper spanning: Does the bridge span the entirety of the page, possibly indicating an intense immersion in the treatment experience?

Labeling: Images with defensive features also tended to contain words or labels.

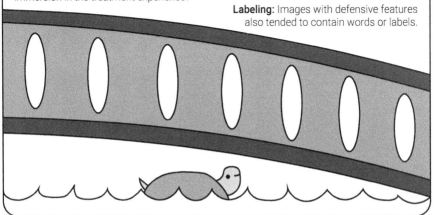

Safe Place

In this intervention, art therapists encourage clients to imagine a safe place and then create that environment, typically by using drawing or painting materials.[57]

Art therapists may ask clients to participate in a relaxation technique, in which they close their eyes and visualize a safe place.

Clients are encouraged to think of elements that make up a safe place.

Some prompts might be:

- What do you need in order to be or feel safe?
- What are some of your comfort items?
- Do you feel safer inside or outside?
- What time of day do you feel most safe?

Clients may be asked to write these elements down or verbally describe them to the art therapist.

From there, clients can create a tangible version of their safe place by using art materials.

This directive may be especially helpful for clients who have experienced trauma, clients in the middle of a transition, clients with anxiety, and clients who are working on safety planning.

Islands

In this directive, clients create their own islands by using drawing, painting, or sculpting materials. It may be helpful for the art therapist to provide suggestions of what to have on their island.[58]

The discussion afterward would involve the location of the island, as well as the general atmosphere. For example, is the island calming or is it dangerous? What are the benefits or disadvantages of living there?

The art therapist and client can then explore the client's "ideal" island and how it is similar or different from their current living situation.

The conversation can then proceed to ways to create a more ideal home environment.

This can also turn into interactive work. Group members can choose to connect everyone's islands or symbolically visit each other's islands.[59]

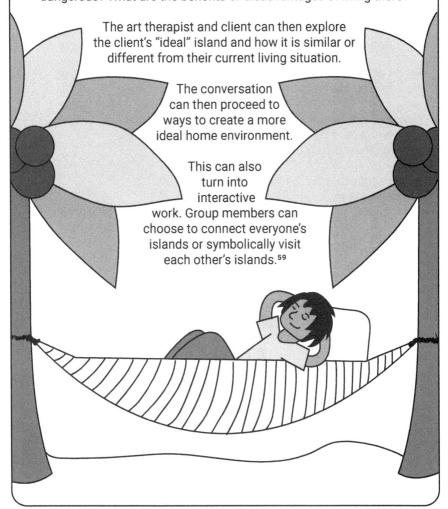

Road Drawings

Michael Hanes discussed roads as metaphors in art therapy.[60] He encouraged clients to draw a picture of a road. As needed, he offered suggestions to help clients begin their drawings.

For example...

- Is the road curved or straight?
- Are there multiple roads or multiple lanes?
- What is the road made out of?
- Where does the road lead?

Hanes offered 12x18" white paper and a variety of drawing materials for clients to create their road.

However, this can be altered, depending on the population. Most two- and three-dimensional materials would work well for rendering or constructing a road.

Hanes suggested the road as a metaphor for life. The road may represent one's past, present, and/or future.

A similar technique involves mapping out one's goals by using the theme of a road map.[61]

Amusement Park Technique

Hrenko and Willis described the Amusement Park Technique, in which participants are invited to "draw an amusement park ride, booth, or event which represents their life."[62]

The authors explained that many of the amusement park choices provide symbolism for individuals with mental health disorders, and they emphasized substance abuse disorders. For example:[63]

Roller Coaster
Ups and downs correlate with the highs and lows of cocaine addiction and/or symptoms of bipolar disorder.

Ferris Wheel
Downward movement is similar to depression.

Merry-Go-Round or Ferris Wheel
Cycles of depression and drinking.

This technique is often used in group settings in which members work on a collaborative mural; each member makes a drawing of their chosen ride.

Patients may discuss relatable feelings of wanting to get off the ride while seemingly having no control over it; someone else is operating the ride. Group members can offer suggestions on how to get off the ride by sharing previous experiences.

Open Studio

Open studio art therapists typically recognize the need for self-expression in the community. Art making is viewed as a process to improve social and personal well-being, not to alleviate any particular symptom or problem. Open studios are therefore informal and individuals do not need to meet any particular criteria to participate.[64]

Buchalter listed the following factors for an effective open studio:[65]

• A safe, creative environment

• The ability of the group leader to facilitate the use of art materials and techniques into a flexible and often non-traditional manner

• Training and experience working with the population involved in the open art studio

Introduction to Art Therapy Assessments

Before we get started on describing specific art-based assessments, let's touch on some important details.

It is important for art therapists to avoid pathologizing clients and projecting their ideas onto clients' artwork. There is no empirical evidence that any single art product is reliable for formal diagnosis.

So, why bother with assessment?

Art therapists use assessments to gain insight about their clients!

Schmanke noted that the following actions need to occur for art-based assessments to be effective:[1]

• Observe the client making the art.
• Involve the client in a discussion of the art.
• Use a variety of client drawings rather than only one for assessment purposes (including free drawings in the assessment collection).

Assessments provide information so art therapists can create treatment plans or decide on further assessment options. Assessments can be used as therapeutic interventions and, if administered throughout the course of therapy, can gauge clients' progress.

I see! So art therapy assessments can be quite valuable!

Art-Based Assessments

Those unfamiliar with art-based assessments may think that art therapists use a "cookbook" approach.[2] In other words, they may think that certain images correlate with symptoms or diagnoses, so art therapists can simply look up clients' images to interpret their artwork.

This approach would disregard the importance of observing clients' behaviors and understanding their interpretation of the artwork.[3] The cookbook approach would also abandon the need to take cultural considerations into account.[4]

So, if I drew a picture of an alligator, you wouldn't be able to say what that means for me psychologically?

Right. Maybe the alligator has meaning for you, but I need to observe your process and listen to your interpretation!

Types of Art Therapy Assessments

Betts divided art therapy assessments into four different domains:[5]

Clinical Interview

Gathering information from several sources about one client

Assessment of Relationship Dynamics

Evaluating dynamics for couples, families, and groups

Cognitive/Neuropsychological and Developmental Evaluation

Identifying indicators of development

Tools that Address Various Realms of Treatment

Collecting information to use for treatment planning and developing therapeutic goals

We will use these domains to organize the assessments in this book. So, we'll start with a few clinical interviews!

Ulman Personality Assessment (UPAP)

The Ulman Personality Assessment helps therapists understand clients' personalities and emotional states.[6]

Administration

Each of the following four tasks is created on a separate sheet of grey paper:

1. Draw anything you'd like.

2. Practice big sweeping motions in the air with your arms. Then recreate those movements with chalk pastel on paper.

Materials

Grey paper 18x24"

12 pack of chalk pastels

Drawing board

24x30" easel

Masking tape

Stopwatch

3. With your eyes closed, draw a large scribble on the paper. Find an image in the scribble. Add details to emphasize that image.

4. Create a drawing based on the scribble.

The first thing I thought of was a pig! I'm not sure why!

First Drawing

Ulman Personality Assessment (UPAP)

Second Drawing

Third Drawing

The scribble in my last drawing reminded me of a man with a top hat and a cape!

Hmm... I wonder if he likes pigs!

Fourth Drawing

Interpretation

After all four drawings are complete, the therapist hangs them on a wall for the client and therapist to view. The therapist asks about the client's associations and perceptions of each of the drawings and of the series as a whole. Therapists observe the use of color and line quality, as well as the client's ability to think and work abstractly.

Diagnostic Drawing Series (DDS)

Barry M. Cohen developed the Diagnostic Drawing Series (DDS),[7] an assessment used mostly with adolescents and adults. The DDS was designed to gather information by observing clients while they participate in structured and unstructured drawing tasks.

Materials
A set of 12 Alphacolor square pastels
Three sheets of 18x24" (60lb) white drawing paper
Krylon Crystal Clear spray fixative

Administration

The DDS has three drawing tasks, all of which are 15 minutes long. Each drawing should be made on a separate sheet of paper, but the client can turn the paper in any direction they wish.

The following are the three directives:[8]

1. "Make a picture using these materials."

2. "Draw a picture of a tree."

3. "Make a picture of how you're feeling, using lines, shapes, and colors."

Diagnostic Drawing Series (DDS)

Interpreting the drawings of the DDS involves using the DDS guide to rate 23 categories of variables.[9]

The Drawing Analysis Form guides the interviewer in rating the "structural level" which includes the formal elements of the drawings, such as line quality, use of color, and composition.[10]

The Drawing Inquiry is used to explore drawings' content, such as the narrative and the symbolism individuals included.

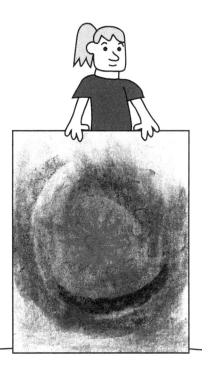

The tasks were designed to give therapists a better understanding of clients' defenses and strengths.[11]

Rubin Diagnostic Interview

Judith Rubin's Diagnostic Interview is an open-ended approach to assessment, in which the client chooses where to work, what materials to work with, and what to create.[12]

In this assessment, children structure the interview themselves. Rubin noted that this process makes the interview less threatening and more enjoyable.

The administrator observes...

Where the children work
- Do they move to different surfaces?
- Where are they in relation to the interviewer?

The product
- Do they speak about the art product?
- What symbolism is present?

Materials
Drawing paper
Fluid media
Drawing tools
Wood scraps
Glue
Cardboard
Tape
Scissors
Clay

Surfaces
Individuals get to choose between working on...

A rectangular table
An easel
The floor

....or a combination of all three!

I love being able to work on the floor! Do you like my purple dragon?

Family Art Assessment

Helen Landgarten developed the Family Art Assessment in 1981. This assessment helps therapists better understand family dynamics by observing how family members interact.[13]

This assessment was made up of three tasks:

Nonverbal Team Art Task
The family divided into partners. Each pairing created artwork without speaking to one another.

Nonverbal Family Art Task
The family as a whole created artwork without speaking to one another.

Verbal Family Art Task
The family as a whole unit created artwork while speaking to one another.

Landgarten encouraged each family member to choose one color to work with for the duration of the session. This way, the therapist could see more clearly which family member created which imagery.

Family Art Evaluation

Hanna Kwiatkowska developed the Family Art Evaluation (FAE) to help art therapists better understand family dynamics.[14]

The assessment consists of six drawings completed with chalk pastels:

1. A free drawing
2. A family portrait
3. An abstract family portrait
4. A scribble drawing
5. A joint family scribble
6. A free drawing

After each drawing, the family is asked to title and sign their work. For the joint drawings, family members come up with a title together and figure out how to sign their work.

Harriet Wadeson modified the FAE to use with couples. This included a family portrait, an abstract portrait of the relationship, a joint scribble, and a self-portrait given to and altered by the spouse.[15]

Family-Centered Circle Drawings (FCCD)

Robert Burns designed Family-Centered Circle Drawings (FCCD) to increase understanding of the relationships between clients and their parents.[16]

Administration

There are three drawings:

1. Mother-centered
2. Father-centered
3. Self-centered

Materials
8.5x11" paper with pre-drawn circle
Drawing materials

Burns provided this directive:

"Draw your mother in the center of the circle. Visually free associate with drawn symbols around the periphery of the circle. Try to draw a whole person, not a stick or cartoon figure."[17]

These directions are then repeated, using father and then self in the center of the circle.

Interpretation

Art therapists observe the size of the figures, the omission or emphasis of body parts, and facial expressions. They also note any patterns in the symbols created around each person.

Kinetic Family Drawing (K-F-D)

Robert Burns and S. Harvard Kaufman developed the Kinetic Family Drawing assessment.[18] This assessment aims to evaluate children's self-concept, development, and personal relationships.[19]

Administration

Burns and Kaufman used this directive when administering the assessment:

Materials

8.5x11" white drawing paper

#2 (HB) pencil

"Draw a picture of everyone in your family doing something, including you doing something. Try to draw whole people, not cartoons or stick people. Remember, make everyone doing something—some kind of action."[20]

The K-F-D comes with an analysis sheet that consists of the following items: styles, symbols, actions of figures, actions between individuals, location of self, and characteristics of figures.

The following are listed under the characteristics of figures category: arm extensions, elevated figures, erasures, figures on back, hanging, omission of body parts, picasso eyes, rotated figures, and K-F-D grid.

Kinetic Family Drawing (K-F-D)

Burns and Kaufman noted that some characteristics of a Kinetic Family Drawing may be a sign of certain concerns.[21] For example:

Characteristic	**MIGHT** indicate	Concern
Long, powerful arms	⟶	A need for control
Prominent teeth	⟶	Anger
Long feet	⟶	A need for security
Shading or scribbling	⟶	Fixation or anxiety
Compartmentalization (separating with boxes)	⟶	Social withdrawal from family members
Lining bottom of paper	⟶	Instability in the home
Underlining figures	⟶	Instability with the figure

219

Bird's Nest Drawing

The Bird's Nest Drawing assesses attachment security and home life.[22]

Administration

In this assessment, the administrator asks the client to "draw a bird's nest."

After the individual completes the drawing, the administrator asks them to write or tell a short story about their bird's nest.

Materials

8.5x11" white drawing paper

10 colors of fine-point markers

The administrator also asks the client to write a title on the front.

There is no age limit for this assessment, though it may be particularly beneficial in assessing children with attachment disorders or who have non-traditional living arrangements.

Bird's Nest Drawing

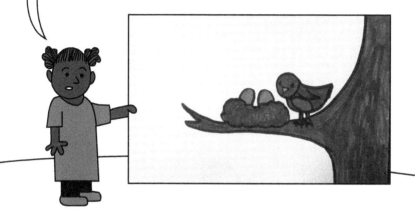

Once upon a time, there was a robin named Bobbin who had two blue eggs. Bobbin patiently waited for the eggs to hatch. One day, they hatched and Bobbin was a proud father bird. The end.

The following elements present in a bird's nest drawing are likely to indicate a secure home:

- Birds in the nest
- Four or more colors
- Green as the dominant color
- The entire bird family
- The nest placed in a tree
- The nest from a profile view, not a bird's eye view
- An entire tree

The administrator uses the Attachment Rating Scale to score the drawing and story. Each question can earn a score of 1–5. These are the questions:[23]

- Are there contents within the nest?
- Does the environment look supportive?
- How sturdy is the nest?
- Does the story about the nest reflect a theme of security or attachment?
- Is a parental nesting animal included?

Kinetic School Drawing

Howard Knoff and H. Thompson Prout developed the Kinetic School Drawing for use with school age children. This assessment aimed to identify a child's family and school relationships.[24]

Administration

Knoff and Prout used the following directive:[25]

"I'd like you to draw a school picture. Put yourself, your teacher, and a friend or two in the picture. Make everyone doing something. Try to draw whole people and make the best drawing you can. Remember, draw yourself, your teacher, and a friend or two, and make everyone doing something."

Interpretation and Scoring

When the picture is complete, the therapist asks what is occurring in the picture and what the figures are doing. The therapist observes the actions occurring between figures, as well as the figures' characteristics and positions to gain insight on the client's school-related relationships.

Kramer Art Assessment

Edith Kramer utilized an evaluation session to learn about clients ages 4 to 15. In this assessment, the art therapist invites children to use three different materials to create images of their choice.[26]

Administration

The first set of materials is a soft pencil, an eraser, and an 8.5x11" piece of paper. When the child has completed their drawing, they are offered either paint or clay.

For the painting task, clients use poster paints in a tray. An empty tray for mixing and grey paper were offered, as well.

Kramer was very specific about the number of paint colors to arrange for the child. For the sake of brevity, we will skip this part, but do look it up yourself!

For the sculpture activity, the art therapist provided clay and simple tools. Once the child finished sculpting, they were invited to paint their creation.

While there is no formal scoring, art therapists should take note of the sequence of materials used and the conversations that took place, as well as the behaviors and attitudes of the child.

Kramer chose the materials specifically to elicit different responses. For example, she noted:

- Pencil drawings typically invited controlled expression and storytelling.
- Painting encouraged more spontaneous expression of affect.
- Clay invited regression and playfulness.

House-Tree-Person Test (H-T-P)

John Buck designed the House-Tree-Person Test to better understand individuals' personality characteristics and interpersonal relationships.[27]

Administration

There are two forms of the test: a chromatic and an achromatic version. The client begins with the achromatic test by using pencils.

Buck wrote the following script:

<table>
<tr><td>Materials</td></tr>
<tr><td>Six sheets of 7x8.5" paper</td></tr>
<tr><td>Several #2 (HB) pencils with erasers</td></tr>
<tr><td>An 8-color set of wax crayons</td></tr>
<tr><td>A stopwatch</td></tr>
<tr><td>H-T-P Scoring Folder</td></tr>
</table>

"Take one of these pencils, please. I want you to draw me as good a picture of a house as you can. You may draw any kind of house you wish, it's entirely up to you. You may erase as much as you like, it will not be counted against you. And you may take as long as you wish, just draw me as good a house as you can."[28]

The script is the same for the tree and the person drawing. But, of course, make sure to trade out the word "house" for "tree" and "person," respectively. Place the sheet of paper horizontally for the house and vertically for the tree and person drawings.

The chromatic version of the test is the same, except the client uses a set of crayons that includes red, orange, yellow, green, blue, purple, brown, and black.

Administration always follows the same order: House, Tree, Person.

So H–T–P and not P–T–H… or T–H–P… or P–H–T…

I think they get it!

House-Tree-Person Test (H-T-P)

The post-drawing interrogation, which consists of 60 questions, occurs after the client has completed all the drawings.[29] Interpretation of the drawings consists of observing details that are present or absent. Let's take a closer look.

The house may indicate aspects of an individual's home or family life.

For example, including a chimney may symbolize warmth in the home, while excluding windows may represent hostility.

The tree may determine characteristics of an individual's unconscious personality.[30]

For example, a small tree may represent feeling insignificant, while excessive shading on the tree may indicate aggressive behaviors.

The person may be indicative of an individual's conscious personality.

For example, if the person's head is especially large, it may indicate a preoccupation with internal fantasy, while the absence of arms may represent perceived inadequacy or helplessness.

Human Figure Drawing Test (HFD)

Elizabeth Koppitz developed the Human Figure Drawing Test (HFD) in 1968.[31] The test's purpose was to determine young clients' developmental levels and to better understand their personalities.[32]

Administration

The directive for this assessment is as follows:

"On this piece of paper, I would like you to draw a WHOLE person. It can be any kind of a person you want to draw, just make sure that it is a whole person and not a stick figure or a cartoon figure."[33]

Materials
White 8.5x11" paper
#2 (HB) pencil
Eraser

Individuals can use as much time as they need to complete the drawing.

The therapist observes the following aspects while the client creates:

The sequence in which the figure was completed

Affect

Spontaneous comments

Behavioral changes

To score the assessment, Koppitz identified 30 items for development and 30 emotional indicators.

Draw A Person Test

Naglieri, McNeish, and Bardos created the Draw A Person test to evaluate emotional difficulties in children and adolescents.[34]

Administration

The therapist asks the client to draw the best picture of a man that they can. This follows with a drawing of a woman and then a picture of themselves.
Clients are given five minutes to complete each drawing.

Materials

Pencil with eraser
Paper

Scoring

There are two groups of items to observe:

- Items involving the figures' dimensions (size, slant, and placement)
- Content, including shading and erasures

Person Picking an Apple from a Tree

Viktor Lowenfeld was the first to describe the drawing of "a person picking an apple from a tree," or the PPAT. Linda Gantt and Carmello Tabone realized that projective assessments would never be an accurate or researchable way to assess psychiatric diagnoses. They developed and applied the Formal Elements Art Therapy Scale (FEATS) to measure objective variables in individuals' PPAT drawings.[35]

Administration

The instructions are simple. The administrator asks the client to "draw a picture of a person picking an apple from a tree."

Materials

12x18" white drawing paper

12 colors of scented markers

If the individual asks if they should draw a man or a woman, the administrator emphasizes the word "person."

The individual chooses how to orient his or her paper.

Person Picking an Apple from a Tree

When the individual has finished the drawing, the administrator uses the FEATS manual to score elements present in the artwork. The FEATS manual provides examples of PPAT drawings so administrators can use them to compare to the client's drawing.

The FEATS scales are:[36]

1. Prominence of Color	6. Logic	11. Line Quality
2. Color Fit	7. Realism	12. Person
3. Implied Energy	8. Problem-solving	13. Rotation
4. Space	9. Developmental Level	14. Perseveration
5. Integration	10. Details	

Each scale can be rated 0–5 or between any of those numbers.

The scales may correlate with symptoms of major depression, bipolar disorder, schizophrenia, and cognitive disorders.

For example, Gantt's research indicated:

- Individuals with depression typically use less color.
- Clients with acute schizophrenia may score low on the logic scale.
- Individuals with organic mental disorders are more likely to use warm colors.[37]

Face Stimulus Assessment (FSA)

The Face Stimulus Assessment (FSA) was developed by Donna Betts as a projective drawing assessment to better understand clients' cognitive and developmental levels.[38] The test was used with "individuals from multicultural backgrounds with multiple disabilities, communication disorders, and autism."[39]

Administration

The administrator arranges the markers randomly.

The FSA is made up of three drawings. For all three tasks, the administrator states, "use the markers and this piece of paper."[40]

Materials

Three pieces of 8.5x11" white paper

Eight Crayola classic markers

Eight Crayola multicultural markers

The difference in tasks involves the pre-drawn images on the paper.

The paper for the first task features an image of a human face.

The paper for the second task features an outline of the face.

The last piece of paper is blank.

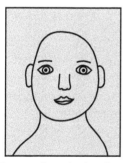 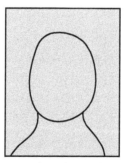 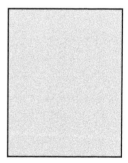

After each task, the drawing is placed out of the client's vision. The assessment takes about 50 minutes to complete.

Face Stimulus Assessment (FSA)

The FSA has quantitative and qualitative rating scales.

The quantitative rating scale utilized nine of the FEATS scales:[41]	The qualitative scale is based on the administrator's observations:[42]
Prominence of color	Motor ability
Details of objects and environment	Realistic colors
Developmental level	Details
Color fit	Adjusting the face to look like self
Implied energy	Use of space within the picture
Logic	Background
Realism	Color differentiation between face and background
Line quality	
Perseveration	

Overall, the assessment was meant to determine how accurately one organizes the human face and retains information.

Silver Drawing Test (SDT)

Rawley Silver drew from Jean Piaget's work to design the Silver Drawing Test (SDT).[43] The SDT assesses for sequential concepts, spatial concepts, and association and formation of concepts. Silver developed the SDT to bypass verbal language and therefore to create a level playing field for all participants.

The Silver Drawing Test is made up of three subtests:[44]

Materials

Assessment booklet

A pencil

Three cylinders and a pebble

1. Predictive Drawing: Requires the participant to predict sequencing, horizontality, and verticality

2. Drawing from Observation: Involves the ability to draw a still life from observation

3. Drawing from Imagination: Encourages the client to choose two pictures to include in a visual story

Administration

The art therapist typically encourages participants to read the instructions and complete the subtests. If necessary, the therapist can read the instructions out loud.

Silver Drawing Test (SDT)

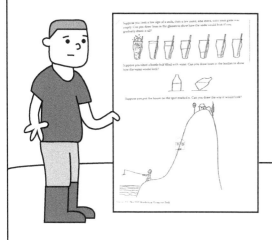

Scoring for the predictive drawing section reflects clients' ability to understand sequential order, as well as horizontality and verticality.[45]

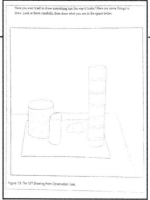

Scoring for the drawing from observation subtest gives insight on how individuals grasp spatial concepts.[46]

The last subtest examines three areas:

1. Emotional content

Strongly negative
to strongly positive themes

2. Self-image

Morbid fantasy to wish-fulfilling fantasy

3. Use of humor

Strongly aggressive humor
to playful humor

Cognitive Art Therapy Assessment (CATA)

Ellen Horovitz developed the Cognitive Art Therapy Assessment (CATA), an open studio approach to a clinical interview. Horovitz designed the CATA as a pre-test/post-test so she could identify changes in development and cognition.[47]

Materials

Pencil, paint, clay, soft pencil, eraser

White 8x11" paper, white 18x24" paper

Set of poster paint (excluding orange, violet, green, and brown)

Container for mixing paints

An empty tray for mixing additional colors

Ceramic clay, clay tools, container for clay slip, container for water

Administration

Horovitz provided a variety of supplies to work with, including drawing materials, painting materials, and clay. She asked with which materials the client would like to begin.

While the participant chooses and works with the materials, the art therapist asks about the participant's familiarity with each one.

Cognitive Art Therapy Assessment (CATA)

Horovitz suggested the following considerations when observing and writing the results for the Cognitive Art Therapy Assessment.[48]

Drawing

- Developmental stage
- Perceptual problems
- Thought disorder
- Motor coordination
- Reality perception
- · Family dynamics

Color

- Affect/Mood
- Response to the excitement of color

Clay

- Capacity for integration
- Propensity for specific kinds of regression
- Capacity to reintegrate after initial regression

Art therapists also observe the formal qualities of the artwork, the subject matter, and the clients' behaviors and attitudes for the duration of the assessment.

LECATA

The Levick Emotional and Cognitive Art Therapy Assessment (LECATA)[49] was first implemented in the Miami-Dade County Public Schools, but the assessment has since been used in multiple countries. The assessment is most often used in school settings.

Administration

The LECATA is made up of five different drawings.

1. A free drawing

2. A picture of the client at their current age

3. A scribble which is then turned into an image

4. A place that is important

5. A family drawing

Check out all my drawings!

The administrator uses the LECATA manual to score both cognitive and emotional scores, which are based on typical development. The scores are shared with faculty and parents during individualized education program (IEP) meetings so the team can identify the student's educational needs, as well as appropriate interventions.

Bender-Gestalt II

Laura Bender produced the original Visual Motor Gestalt Test in 1938.[50] The current test, Bender-Gestalt II, aims to gain a better understanding of individuals' visuomotor perceptions, developmental level, and neuropsychological development by inviting clients to reproduce designs.[51]

Administration

The most recent edition has 16 designs for two different tests, one for ages 8 and under, and one for ages 8 and older.[52] The newest edition also had a recall test for individuals to recreate images from memory.

Materials

Bender-Gestalt II Test Kit
Paper
Pencil

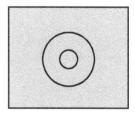

Scoring

There is a five point scale for reproducing designs:[53]

0—No resemblance/lack of design
1—Slight, vague resemblance
2—Some, moderate resemblance
3—Close resemblance
4—Nearly perfect

Motor test:

1—Line touches both end points and does not leave the box. Line may touch the border but cannot go over it.
0—Line extends outside the box or does not touch both end points.
Twelve points are possible.

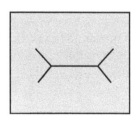

Perceptual test:

Each correct response gets a point; ten points are possible.

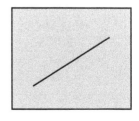

Magazine Photo Collage (MPC)

Helen Landgarten designed the Magazine Photo Collage as a multicultural assessment to better understand clients' conflicts and defenses.[54]

Administration:[55]

Clients move through the following steps with prompting from the art therapist.

Look through a box of collage materials and select any images that resonate with you. Paste the image(s) onto paper and write or speak about anything that comes to mind.

Materials

Newsprint or white paper, 16x20"

Thin black marker

Medium black marker

Ball point pen

Round tip scissors

Lead pencil

Liquid glue

Choose six images of people and paste them onto paper. Then write or speak about what the people are thinking and saying.

Select another six images from the box, those that represent good and bad things. Again, paste the images and then write or speak about them.

Choose an image of a person. After pasting the picture down, write or speak about what is happening to them and if the situation will change. If the situation will change, then find an image to represent what will make the change. Paste that image down, as well.

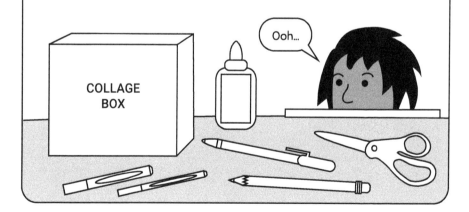

Magazine Photo Collage (MPC)

Observation

The therapist observes how the client handled the collage material. For example, were the pictures torn or trimmed, or were they left alone? How was the glue handled, and did the placement of images appear random or more controlled?[56]

The therapist also notes the pictorial content and if any particular messages or patterns appeared.[57]

The completed collage helps the therapist gather information through the meaning of the images; this insight may help the therapist develop appropriate and effective interventions.[58]

Draw-a-Person-in-the-Rain (DAPR)

Emanuel Hammer described the task "Draw-a-Person-in-the-Rain" in 1958.[59] Verinis, Lichtenberg, and Henrich found correlations between specific elements in these drawings and the artist's level of and ability to cope with stress.[60]

Administration:

The facilitator asks the client to "draw a person in the rain as best you can."[61] The patient has ten minutes to complete the drawing.

Materials

8.5x11" white paper

Two #2 (HB) pencils with erasers

When the drawing is complete, the therapist may ask questions about the person in the drawing, including how they are feeling and how they are coping with life's stressors.

The amount and/or intensity of the rain may be symbolic of the client's external stress, while the level of protection (such as an umbrella or a shelter) may indicate one's ability to cope with stress.[62]

I have a lot of stress, but I'm coping with it well!

Belief Art Therapy Assessment (BATA)

The Belief Art Therapy Assessment (BATA) was developed by Ellen Horovitz to understand one's sense of spirituality. Horovitz recommended that the Belief Art Therapy Assessment only be used when a client brings up beliefs and/or questions them.[63]

Administration[64]

Horovitz began the assessment by asking, "Have you ever thought about how the universe was created and who or what was responsible for that creation?" After that, two directives were given.

1. "Many people believe in a God; if you also have a belief in God, would you draw, paint, or sculpt what God means to you?"

2. "Some people believe that there is an opposite of God and/or what they believe in. If you believe there is an opposite force, could you also draw, paint, or sculpt the meaning of that?"

This approach helps the therapist and client engage in discussion about spirituality. Individuals may gain understanding of their spirituality and how it contributes to their overall health and well-being.

Art Therapy Dream Assessment (ATDA)

Ellen Horovitz developed the Art Therapy Dream Assessment (ATDA) in 1999 to increase understanding of clients' treatment goals and to help the client resolve emotional conflicts.[65]

Administration

To begin, the art therapist asks the client to choose one of their dreams that stood out to them in some way.

Horovitz offered a variety of two- and three-dimensional materials for clients to use. The client goes through the following steps:[66]

1. Use the materials to illustrate the dream.
2. Write a paragraph about the dream.
3. Read the paragraph. Therapist then reads the paragraph out loud.
4. Choose important words from the dream and underline them.
5. Read the underlined words. Therapist then reads the words out loud.
6. Out of the underlined words, circle the most important ones.
7. Read the new words. Therapist then reads the words out loud.
8. Reduce the number of words to eight.
9. Therapist reads the eight words out loud.
10. Use eight words in a sentence.
11. Client reads the sentence. Therapist then reads the sentence.

Where are my teeth?!

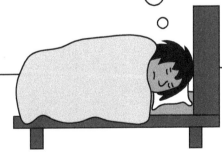

The dream and words chosen provide insight on the client's emotional needs.

Computer Technology Integration

Seong-in Kim noted that computer algorithms could help art therapists analyze formal elements of drawing assessments to quantify the information and improve efficiency in scoring.[67]

Computer systems can score traditional drawing tests, but Kim believed computer-based assessments may also be created. These could be either traditional tests altered for the digital realm or entirely new assessments.

Kim explained that computer rating systems could provide more accurate information for the following variables.[68]

Variables

- Number of colors and color list

- Area colored

- Number of clusters

- Area of colored convex hull

- Length of edges

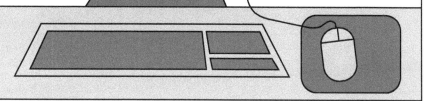

Kim pointed out that the goal of using computer rating systems is not to replace human raters. Instead, they would give humans more opportunity to focus on observing the nuances during the art-making process that require a human's judgment.

A Quick Word about Assessments

There is not yet enough research to demonstrate reliability or validity of art therapy assessments. Art-based assessments do not yield diagnoses; they are a means to gather more information about clients.[69]

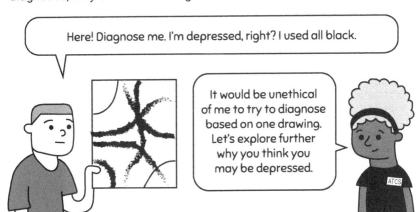

Another note before you move to the last chapter. Many of the assessments presented here require additional training in order to accurately administer and score.[70]

245

Summary

In this section, we will describe what it means to be an art therapist and provide resources for additional information.

Characteristics and Actions

Junge and Newall collected "letters to a young art therapist" from movers and shakers in the field. The writers identified the following characteristics and actions as important in becoming an effective art therapist.[2]

Problem–solving
Taking care of oneself
Having a sense of humor
Showing compassion
Sandra Graves-Alcorn

Learning throughout one's lifetime
Arthur Robbins

Being respectful
Being okay with mistakes
Giving and accepting criticism
Demonstrating passion for art
Catherine Hyland Moon

Being aware of discrimination
Committing to social advocacy
Cliff Joseph

Engaging in research
Frances Kaplan

Articulating the profession to others
Admitting what one doesn't know
Thinking for oneself
Collaborating with other clinicians
Being okay with mistakes
Accepting all clients
Finding ways to restore oneself
Judith Aron Rubin

Writing clearly about
the profession
Cathy Malchiodi

Finding humor
Showing leadership
Speaking with passion
Demonstrating bravery
Maxine Junge

Creating personal art
Being okay with mistakes
Shaun McNiff

Multicultural Competence

Art therapists are likely to work with individuals from a variety of different cultural backgrounds, so multicultural competence and sensitivity are crucial in art therapy practice.[3]

To be effective, art therapists must have an understanding of cultural differences between themselves and their clients. One of the first steps for any mental health professional is to gain self-awareness about their own culture so they do not impose their values and beliefs on the client.[4] This will also help the professional identify their biases so they do not negatively affect the therapeutic relationship.[5]

Of course, it is also helpful to understand clients' cultural backgrounds, including how their race, class, and gender have affected their experiences.[6] It is also important to note that diverse cultures have varying opinions and perceptions of therapy. In general, art therapists aim to work within the client's value system.[7]

Social Action

Beyond serving clients directly in sessions, art therapists have a "responsibility to raise awareness, correct power imbalances, and, when necessary, be advocates for social justice."[8]

Kaplan listed the following factors of social action art therapy.[9]

Understanding origins of socially unacceptable behavior

RATh

Creating social change

RATh

Providing community service

ATR-BC

Instruction in socially oriented interactions

ATCS

Increasing awareness of social problems

ATR

Increasing sensitivity to the social context of troubled individuals

ATR

Identity

The following are a few perspectives regarding an art therapist's identity.

Bob Ault

"A good art therapist is like a skater. One skate is an understanding of art and the other is an understanding of people, of psychology and counseling... Sometimes you push off with one skate, sometimes you push off with the other. And sometimes you glide along on both."[10]

Marcia Rosal

"Some of us may create more art than others, some of us may do more research than others, some of us may be more inclined to use more art or, conversely, more verbal clinical skills in therapy sessions than others. But these differences do not mean that any of us are lesser art therapists than others."[11]

Charlotte Boston

"A mosaic is defined as art consisting of a design made of small pieces of colored stone or glass. As an art therapist, I have a 'mosaic' of roles, each of which is a part that contributes to the whole image and design of who I am. I am an artist, therapist, clinician, facilitator, educator, and nurturer."[12]

Don Jones

"Ongoing engagement in art expression is an essential part of our vocation and continuing personal and professional identity. Art is our way of growing in self-awareness and insight, personally and as therapists. It is the tool for understanding our clients. We can find inspiration and ever new and changing dynamic in our work. It is dishonest to ask our clients to do anything that we have not or will not do or are not doing ourselves."[13]

David Gussak

"We need to shout from the hilltops that to be an art therapist requires a specialized education; that is, a combination of clinical, medical, rehabilitation, and—most importantly—art."[14]

Judith Rubin

"I think a competent art therapist is true to both Art and Therapy and puts them together in a way that seems best suited to meet the needs of whomever they are serving at the moment."[15]

Art Therapy Programs in the United Kingdom

In both the United Kingdom and the United States, art therapists must earn their master's degrees before practicing. The following is a list of approved master's programs in the United Kingdom.[16] The next page features approved and accredited programs in the United States.

Be sure to visit baat.org to view the most current list of programs!

University of Ulster | Belfast
University of Chester | Chester
University of Derby | Derby
Queen Margaret University | Edinburgh
University of Hertfordshire | Hatfield
Goldsmiths | London
The Institute for Arts in Therapy and Education (IATE) | London
University of Roehampton | London
Art Therapy Northern Programme | Sheffield
University of South Wales | Wales

Wow! Who knew there were so many programs? How do hopeful art therapists ever decide where to apply?

A good idea is to browse the universities' websites and do some reading on the programs. Another helpful step is to reach out to program directors and leaders. Of course, a lot of information can be found on the websites of the British Association of Art Therapists and the American Art Therapy Association.

Art Therapy Programs in the United States

In the United States, the American Art Therapy Association's Educational Program Approval Board (EPAB) is being phased out and replaced by external accrediting bodies, like the Commission on Accreditation of Allied Health Education Programs (CAAHEP). **Be sure to check out arttherapy.org to view the most current list of programs!**

Albertus Magnus College | New Haven, CT
The George Washington University | Alexandria, DC
Florida State University | Tallahassee, FL
Southern Illinois University Edwardsville | Edwardsville, IL
St. Mary-of-the-Woods College | St. Mary of the Woods, IN
Emporia State University | Emporia, KS
Long Island University Post Campus | Brookville, NY
New York University | New York, NY
Lewis & Clark College | Portland, OR
Edinboro University | Edinboro, PA
Eastern Virginia Medical School | Norfolk, VA
Antioch University Seattle | Seattle, WA

These are the accredited master's programs.[17]

Notre Dame de Namur University | Belmont, CA
Loyola Marymount University | Los Angeles, CA
Naropa University | Boulder, CO
Adler University | Chicago, IL
School of the Art Institute of Chicago | Chicago, IL
University of Louisville | Louisville, KY
Lesley University | Cambridge, MA
Springfield College | Springfield, MA
Wayne State University | Detroit, MI
Adler Graduate School | Minnetonka, MN
Caldwell University | Caldwell, NJ
Southwestern College | Santa Fe, NM
Pratt Institute | Brooklyn, NY
Hofstra University | Hempstead, NY
School of Visual Arts | New York, NY
College of Mount Saint Vincent | Riverdale, NY
Nazareth College of Rochester | Rochester, NY
Ursuline College | Pepper Pike, OH
Seton Hill University | Greensburg, PA
Drexel University | Philadelphia, PA
Marywood University | Scranton, PA
Mount Mary University | Milwaukee, WI

And these are the approved programs![18] At the time of publication, many of these programs are in the process of achieving external accreditation.

How to Find an Art Therapist (US and UK)

Maybe you're thinking, "Gosh, I don't know if I want to be an art therapist, but I sure would like to enhance my life by participating in art therapy." If so, you're in luck!

The national associations of the United States and the United Kingdom both make it easy to find an art therapist.

To find an art therapist in the United Kingdom

Go to the British Association of Art Therapists (BAAT) website at: https://www.baat.org

Click on the button "Find an Art Therapist" on the home page.

This will take you to a search engine, so you can find practitioners by role, client group, clinical area, and/or area of practice.

To find an art therapist in the United States

Go to the Art Therapy Credentials Board (ATCB) website at: https://atcb.org

Click on the link that says, "Find a Credentialed Art Therapist." This can be found under the "Public" heading.

This will take you to the database of current ATCB credential holders.

Helpful Resources

I am 100% sure that you want to keep learning about art therapy, so here are some wonderful resources to check out. This page features only a small fraction of the art therapy literature out there; be sure to look at the extensive references in the Endnotes!

Journals

Art Therapy: Journal of the American Art Therapy Association

Canadian Art Therapy Association Journal

The International Journal of Art Therapy: Inscape

Websites

American Art Therapy Association | arttherapy.org

Art Therapy Credentials Board, Inc. | atcb.org

Art Therapy Research Information | arttherapy.org/research

British Association of Art Therapists | baat.org

The Health & Care Professions Council | hcpc-uk.org

Institute for Continuing Education in Art Therapy | at-institute.arttherapy.org

Books:

Gussak, D.E. and Rosal, M.L. (2016) *The Wiley Handbook of Art Therapy*. Chichester, UK: John Wiley & Sons.

Liebmann, M. (2004) *Art Therapy for Groups: A Handbook of Themes and Exercises* (2nd ed.). Hove, UK: Routledge.

Malchiodi, C.A. (2012) *Handbook of Art Therapy* (2nd ed.). New York, NY: Guilford Press.

Moon, C.H. (2010) *Materials and Media in Art Therapy: Critical Understandings of Diverse Artistic Vocabularies*. New York, NY: Routledge.

Rubin, J.A. (2010) *Introduction to Art Therapy: Sources and Resources* (2nd ed.). New York, NY: Routledge.

Endnotes

Introduction

1   American Art Therapy Association (2017) "Definition of profession." Retrieved from www.arttherapy.org/upload/2017_DefinitionofProfession.pdf; British Association of Art Therapists (n.d.) "What is art therapy?" Retrieved from www.baat.org/About-Art-Therapy
2   American Art Therapy Association (2017) "Definition of profession." Retrieved from www.arttherapy.org/upload/2017_DefinitionofProfession.pdf
3   Rubin, J.A. (2010) *Introduction to Art Therapy: Sources and Resources* (2nd ed.). New York, NY: Routledge.
4   Garyfalakis, R. (2017) "What's the difference between art therapy and an art class?" Retrieved from www.artastherapy.ca/art-as-therapy-blog/2017/3/14/whats-the-difference-between-art-therapy-and-an-art-class
5   Rubin, J.A. (2010) *Introduction to Art Therapy: Sources and Resources* (2nd ed.). New York, NY: Routledge.
6   British Association of Art Therapists (2016) "Art therapy information." Retrieved from www.baat.org/Assets/Docs/2018%20ART%20THERAPY%20TRAINING%20new%20details.pdf
7   American Art Therapy Association (2017) "Becoming an art therapist." Retrieved from https://arttherapy.org/becoming-art-therapist
8   American Art Therapy Association (2017) "Educational standards." Retrieved from https://arttherapy.org/educational-standards
9   British Association of Art Therapists (2016) "Art therapy information." Retrieved from www.baat.org/Assets/Docs/2018%20ART%20THERAPY%20TRAINING%20new%20details.pdf
10 American Art Therapy Association (2017) "Educational standards." Retrieved from https://arttherapy.org/educational-standards
11 Health & Care Professions Council (2019) "UK application forms." Retrieved from www.hpc-uk.org/registration/getting-on-the-register/uk-applications/uk-application-forms
12 Art Therapy Credentials Board, Inc. (2019) "About the credentials." Retrieved from www.atcb.org/New_Applicants/AboutTheCredentials
13 British Association of Art Therapists (n.d.) "Career information." Retrieved from www.baat.org/Careers-Training/Career-Information
14 American Art Therapy Association (2017) "About art therapy." Retrieved from https://arttherapy.org/about-art-therapy
15 Rubin, J.A. (2010) *Introduction to Art Therapy: Sources and Resources* (2nd ed.). New York, NY: Routledge.
16 Ibid.
17 Moon, C.H. (2010) *Materials and Media in Art Therapy: Critical Understandings of Diverse Artistic Vocabularies*. New York, NY: Routledge.
18 Landgarten, H.B. (1987) *Family Art Psychotherapy: A Clinical Guide and Casebook*. New York, NY: Brunner/Mazel, p.7.
19 Rubin, J.A. (2010) *Introduction to Art Therapy: Sources and Resources* (2nd ed.). New York, NY: Routledge; Moon, C.H. (2010) *Materials and Media in Art Therapy: Critical Understandings of Diverse Artistic Vocabularies*. New York, NY: Routledge.

History

1   Rubin, J.A. (2010) *Introduction to Art Therapy: Sources and Resources* (2nd ed.). New York, NY: Routledge.
2   Ibid., pp.51–57.
3   Ibid., p.54.
4   Ibid.

5   Ibid.
6   Vick, R.M. (2012) "A Brief History of Art Therapy." In C.A. Malchiodi (ed.) *Handbook of Art Therapy* (2nd ed.). New York, NY: Guilford Press.
7   Rubin, J.A. (2010) *Introduction to Art Therapy: Sources and Resources* (2nd ed.). New York, NY: Routledge.
8   Vick, R.M. (2012) "A Brief History of Art Therapy." In C.A. Malchiodi (ed.) *Handbook of Art Therapy* (2nd ed.). New York, NY: Guilford Press.
9   Junge, M.B. (2010) *The Modern History of Art Therapy in the United States*. Springfield, IL: Charles C Thomas.
10 Vick, R.M. (2012) "A Brief History of Art Therapy." In C.A. Malchiodi (ed.) *Handbook of Art Therapy* (2nd ed.). New York, NY: Guilford Press.
11 Taylor & Francis Online (2020) *Canadian Art Therapy Association Journal*. Retrieved from www.tandfonline.com/toc/ucat20/current
12 Vick, R.M. (2012) "A Brief History of Art Therapy." In C.A. Malchiodi (ed.) *Handbook of Art Therapy* (2nd ed.). New York, NY: Guilford Press.
13 Taylor & Francis Online (2020) *International Journal of Art Therapy*. Retrieved from www.tandfonline.com/loi/rart20
14 Junge, M.B. (2010) *The Modern History of Art Therapy in the United States*. Springfield, IL: Charles C. Thomas; Rubin, J.A. (2010) *Introduction to Art Therapy: Sources and Resources* (2nd ed.). New York, NY: Routledge; American Art Therapy Association (2017) "Multicultural sub-committee." Retrieved from https://arttherapy.org/multicultural-sub-committee; British Association of Art Therapists (2020) "Qualifying training courses for art therapists in the UK." Retrieved from www.baat.org/Assets/Docs/2020%20HCPC%20Validated%20Art%20 Therapy%20MA%20Training.pdf; Commission on Accreditation of Allied Health Education Programs (2017) "Find a program." Retrieved from www.caahep.org/Accreditation/Find-a-Program.aspx
15 Junge, M.B. (2010) *The Modern History of Art Therapy in the United States*. Springfield, IL: Charles C. Thomas; Fish, B. (2013) "Reflections on the beginning of the ATCB." *ATCB Review 20*, 2, 1, 9. Retrieved from www.atcb.org/resource/pdf/Newsletter/Summer2013.pdf; American Art Therapy Association (2017) "Credentials and licensure." Retrieved from https://arttherapy.org/credentials-and-licensure
16 American Art Therapy Association (2017) "State advocacy." Retrieved from https://arttherapy.org/state-advocacy

Framework and Models

1   Rubin, J.A. (2010) *Introduction to Art Therapy: Sources and Resources* (2nd ed.). New York, NY: Routledge.
2   Personal communication, L. Schmanke, February 22, 2020.
3   Rubin, J.A. (2011) *The Art of Art Therapy: What Every Art Therapist Needs to Know*. New York, NY: Routledge.
4   Personal communication, L. Schmanke, February 22, 2020.
5   Rubin, J.A. (2011) *The Art of Art Therapy: What Every Art Therapist Needs to Know*. New York, NY: Routledge.
6   Ibid., p.38.
7   Schmanke, L. (2018) "Freud" [Class handout]. Department of Counselor Education, Emporia State University, Emporia, KS.
8   Schmanke, L. (2018) "Mahler" [Class handout]. Department of Counselor Education, Emporia State University, Emporia, KS; Personal communication, L. Schmanke, June 29, 2020.
9   Schmanke, L. (2005) "Erikson's Stages of Psychosocial Development" [Class handout]. Department of Counselor Education, Emporia State University, Emporia, KS.
10 Schmanke, L. (2004) "Piaget's Stages of Cognitive Development" [Class handout]. Department of Counselor Education, Emporia State University, Emporia, KS.
11 Lowenfeld, V. and Brittain, W.L. (1987) *Creative and Mental Growth* (8th ed.). Upper Saddle River, NJ: Prentice-Hall.
12 Rubin, J.A. (2005) *Child Art Therapy* (25th Anniversary ed.). Hoboken, NJ: John Wiley & Sons.

13   Ibid., pp.36–46.
14   Ibid., p.37.
15   Schmanke, L. (2018) "Wrestling with Golomb–Summary Thoughts from Chapter 3" [Class handout]. Department of Counselor Education, Emporia State University, Emporia, KS. Handout based on information from Golomb, C. (2004) *The Child's Creation of a Pictorial World* (2nd ed.). Mahwah, NJ: Lawrence Erlbaum.
16   Kagin, S.L. and Lusebrink, V.B. (1978) "The expressive therapies continuum." *Art Psychotherapy 5*, 171–180.
17   Hinz, L.D. (2009) *Expressive Therapies Continuum: A Framework for Using Art in Therapy*. New York, NY: Routledge.
18   Kagin, S.L. and Lusebrink, V.B. (1978) "The expressive therapies continuum." *Art Psychotherapy 5*, 171–180; Hinz, L.D. (2009) *Expressive Therapies Continuum: A Framework for Using Art in Therapy*. New York, NY: Routledge.
19   "Atom Conceptualization": personal communication, G. Wolf Bordonaro, April 12, 2019.
20   Hinz, L.D. (2009) *Expressive Therapies Continuum: A Framework for Using Art in Therapy*. New York, NY: Routledge; Lusebrink, V.B. (1990) "Levels of Expression and Systems Approach to Therapy." In V.B. Lusebrink (ed.) *Imagery and Visual Expression in Therapy*. Boston, MA: Springer.
21   Aach-Feldman, S. and Kunkle-Miller, C. (2016) "Developmental Art Therapy." In J.A. Rubin (ed.) *Approaches to Art Therapy: Theory and Technique* (3rd ed.). New York, NY: Routledge.
22   Schmanke, L. (2018) "Developmental Art Therapy" [Class handout]. Department of Counselor Education, Emporia State University, Emporia, KS. Handout based on information from Rosal, M.L. (1996) *Approaches to Art Therapy for Children*. Burlingame, CA: Abbeygate.
23   Malchiodi, C.A. (2012) "Developmental Art Therapy." In C.A. Malchiodi (ed.) *Handbook of Art Therapy* (2nd ed.). New York, NY: Guilford Press.

Theories and Approaches

1   Rubin, J.A. (2010) *Introduction to Art Therapy: Sources and Resources* (2nd ed.). New York, NY: Routledge, p.95.
2   Rubin, J.A. (2016) *Approaches to Art Therapy: Theory and Technique* (3rd ed.). New York, NY: Routledge. Rubin organized her book in this way.
3   Rubin, J. (2016) "Discovery and Insight in Art Therapy." In J.A. Rubin (ed.) *Approaches to Art Therapy: Theory and Technique* (3rd ed.). New York, NY: Routledge.
4   Corey, G. (2017) *Theory and Practice of Counseling and Psychotherapy* (10th ed.). Boston, MA: Cengage Learning.
5   Corey, G. (2017) *Theory and Practice of Counseling and Psychotherapy* (10th ed.). Boston, MA: Cengage Learning; Rubin, J.A. (2016) "Psychoanalytic Art Therapy." In D.E. Gussak and M.L. Rosal (eds) *The Wiley Handbook of Art Therapy*. Chichester, UK: John Wiley & Sons.
6   Corey, G. (2017) *Theory and Practice of Counseling and Psychotherapy* (10th ed.). Boston, MA: Cengage Learning.
7   Ibid.
8   Rubin, J.A. (2016) "Discovery and Insight in Art Therapy." In J.A. Rubin (ed.) *Approaches to Art Therapy: Theory and Technique* (3rd ed.). New York, NY: Routledge.
9   Naumburg, M. (1966) *Dynamically Oriented Art Therapy: Its Principles and Practices*. New York, NY: Grune & Stratton.
10   Corey, G. (2017) *Theory and Practice of Counseling and Psychotherapy* (10th ed.). Boston, MA: Cengage Learning.
11   Rubin, J.A. (2016) "Discovery and Insight in Art Therapy." In J.A. Rubin (ed.) *Approaches to Art Therapy: Theory and Technique* (3rd ed.). New York, NY: Routledge.
12   Freud, S. (1989) "The ego and the id (1923)." *TACD Journal 17*, 1, 5–22.
13   Ibid.
14   Ibid.
15   Kramer, E. and Gerity, L.A. (2000) *Art as Therapy: Collected Papers*. London: Jessica Kingsley Publishers.
16   Rubin, J.A. (2016) "Psychoanalytic Art Therapy." In D.E. Gussak and M.L. Rosal (eds) *The Wiley Handbook of Art Therapy*. Chichester, UK: John Wiley & Sons.

17   Rubin, J.A. (2016) "Discovery and Insight in Art Therapy." In J.A. Rubin (ed.) *Approaches to Art Therapy: Theory and Technique* (3rd ed.). New York, NY: Routledge. Inspired by the story of Mrs. L, pp.75–83.
18   Malchiodi, C.A. (2012) "Psychoanalytic, Analytic, and Object Relations Approaches." In C.A. Malchiodi (ed.) *Handbook of Art Therapy* (2nd ed.). New York, NY: Guilford Press; Corey, G. (2017) *Theory and Practice of Counseling and Psychotherapy* (10th ed.). Boston, MA: Cengage Learning.
19   Robbins, A. (2016) "Object Relations and Art Therapy." In J.A. Rubin (ed.) *Approaches to Art Therapy: Theory and Technique* (3rd ed.). New York, NY: Routledge.
20   Malchiodi, C.A. (2012) "Psychoanalytic, Analytic, and Object Relations Approaches." In C.A. Malchiodi (ed.) *Handbook of Art Therapy* (2nd ed.). New York, NY: Guilford Press; Corey, G. (2017) *Theory and Practice of Counseling and Psychotherapy* (10th ed.). Boston, MA: Cengage Learning.
21   Malchiodi, C.A. (2012) "Psychoanalytic, Analytic, and Object Relations Approaches." In C.A. Malchiodi (ed.) *Handbook of Art Therapy* (2nd ed.). New York, NY: Guilford Press, p.71.
22   Corey, G. (2017) *Theory and Practice of Counseling and Psychotherapy* (10th ed.). Boston, MA: Cengage Learning.
23   Jung, C.G. (2014) *The Archetypes and the Collective Unconscious*. New York, NY: Routledge.
24   Ibid.
25   Swan-Foster, N. (2016) "Jungian Art Therapy." In J.A. Rubin (ed.) *Approaches to Art Therapy: Theory and Technique* (3rd ed.). New York, NY: Routledge.
26   Ibid.
27   Rubin, J.A. (2016) "Psychoanalytic Art Therapy." In D.E. Gussak and M.L. Rosal (eds) *The Wiley Handbook of Art Therapy*. Chichester, UK: John Wiley & Sons.
28   Malchiodi, C.A. (2012) "Psychoanalytic, Analytic, and Object Relations Approaches." In C.A. Malchiodi (ed.) *Handbook of Art Therapy* (2nd ed.). New York, NY: Guilford Press.
29   Malchiodi, C.A. (2012) "Psychoanalytic, Analytic, and Object Relations Approaches." In C.A. Malchiodi (ed.) *Handbook of Art Therapy* (2nd ed.). New York, NY: Guilford Press; Corey, G. (2017) *Theory and Practice of Counseling and Psychotherapy* (10th ed.). Boston, MA: Cengage Learning; Swan-Foster, N. (2016) "Jungian Art Therapy." In J.A. Rubin (ed.) *Approaches to Art Therapy: Theory and Technique* (3rd ed.). New York, NY: Routledge.
30   Corey, G. (2017) *Theory and Practice of Counseling and Psychotherapy* (10th ed.). Boston, MA: Cengage Learning.
31   Moon, B. (2016) "Art Therapy: Humanism in Action." In J.A. Rubin (ed.) *Approaches to Art Therapy: Theory and Technique* (3rd ed.). New York, NY: Routledge, p.204.
32   Corey, G. (2017) *Theory and Practice of Counseling and Psychotherapy* (10th ed.). Boston, MA: Cengage Learning; Rogers, C. (1951) *Client-Centered Therapy: Its Current Practice, Implications and Theory*. London: Constable.
33   Rogers, N. (2016) "Person-Centered Expressive Arts Therapy: A Path to Wholeness." In J.A. Rubin (ed.) *Approaches to Art Therapy: Theory and Technique* (3rd ed.). New York, NY: Routledge; Corey, G. (2017) *Theory and Practice of Counseling and Psychotherapy* (10th ed.). Boston, MA: Cengage Learning; Moon, B. (2016) "Art Therapy: Humanism in action." In J.A. Rubin (ed.) *Approaches to Art Therapy: Theory and Technique* (3rd ed.). New York, NY: Routledge.
34   Rogers, C.R. (1969) *Freedom to Learn: A View of What Education Might Become*. Columbus, OH: C.E. Merrill.
35   Corey, G. (2017) *Theory and Practice of Counseling and Psychotherapy* (10th ed.). Boston, MA: Cengage Learning.
36   Rogers, N. (2016) "Person-Centered Expressive Arts Therapy: A Path to Wholeness." In J.A. Rubin (ed.) *Approaches to Art Therapy: Theory and Technique* (3rd ed.). New York, NY: Routledge.
37   Maslow, A.H. (1943) "A theory of human motivation." *Psychological Review 50*, 4, 370–396.
38   Rogers, C.R. (1958) "A process conception of psychotherapy." *American Psychologist 13*, 4, 142–149.
39   Rogers, N. (2016) "Person-Centered Expressive Arts Therapy: A Path to Wholeness." In J.A. Rubin (ed.) *Approaches to Art Therapy: Theory and Technique* (3rd ed.). New York, NY: Routledge.
40   Moon, B. (2016) "Art Therapy: Humanism in action." In J.A. Rubin (ed.) *Approaches to Art Therapy: Theory and Technique* (3rd ed.). New York, NY: Routledge.
41   Kim, S. (2010) "A story of a healing relationship: The person-centered approach in expressive arts therapy." *Journal of Creativity in Mental Health 5*, 1, 93–98. 10.1080/15401381003627350. NOTE: Inspired by the story of Mrs. H.
42   Corey, G. (2017) *Theory and Practice of Counseling and Psychotherapy* (10th ed.). Boston, MA: Cengage Learning.

43 Corey, G. (2017) *Theory and Practice of Counseling and Psychotherapy* (10th ed.). Boston, MA: Cengage Learning; Malchiodi, C.A. (2012) "Humanistic Approaches." In C.A. Malchiodi (ed.) *Handbook of Art Therapy* (2nd ed.). New York, NY: Guilford Press; Moon, B. (2016) "Art Therapy: Humanism in Action." In J.A. Rubin (ed.) *Approaches to Art Therapy: Theory and Technique* (3rd ed.). New York, NY: Routledge.

44 Corey, G. (2017) *Theory and Practice of Counseling and Psychotherapy* (10th ed.). Boston, MA: Cengage Learning, pp.138–146.

45 Corey, G. (2017) *Theory and Practice of Counseling and Psychotherapy* (10th ed.). Boston, MA: Cengage Learning.

46 Ibid.

47 Malchiodi, C.A. (2012) "Humanistic Approaches." In C.A. Malchiodi (ed.) *Handbook of Art Therapy* (2nd ed.). New York, NY: Guilford Press, p.77.

48 Ibid., p.76.

49 Moon, B.L. (2009) *Existential Art Therapy: The Canvas Mirror* (3rd ed.). Springfield, IL: Charles C. Thomas. NOTE: Inspired by "A Story of Overindulgence," pp.194–195.

50 Corey, G. (2017) *Theory and Practice of Counseling and Psychotherapy* (10th ed.). Boston, MA: Cengage Learning; Rhyne, J. (2016) "Gestalt Art Therapy." In J.A. Rubin (ed.) *Approaches to Art Therapy: Theory and Technique* (3rd ed.). New York, NY: Routledge.

51 Amendt-Lyon, N. (2001) "Art and creativity in Gestalt therapy." *Gestalt Review 5*, 4, 225–248.

52 Yalom, I.D. (2002) *The Gift of Therapy: An Open Letter to a New Generation of Therapists and Their Patients*. New York, NY: HarperCollins.

53 Corey, G. (2017) *Theory and Practice of Counseling and Psychotherapy* (10th ed.). Boston, MA: Cengage Learning.

54 Ciornai, S. (2016) "Gestalt Art Therapy: A Path to Consciousness Expansion." In D.E. Gussak and M.L. Rosal (eds) *The Wiley Handbook of Art Therapy*. Chichester, UK: John Wiley & Sons.

55 Corey, G. (2017) *Theory and Practice of Counseling and Psychotherapy* (10th ed.). Boston, MA: Cengage Learning.

56 Polster, E. and Polster, M. (1973) *Gestalt Therapy Integrated: Contours of Theory and Practice*. New York, NY: Brunner/Mazel.

57 Corey, G. (2017) *Theory and Practice of Counseling and Psychotherapy* (10th ed.). Boston, MA: Cengage Learning.

58 Ibid., p.201.

59 Rhyne, J. (2016) "Gestalt Art Therapy." In J.A. Rubin (ed.) *Approaches to Art Therapy: Theory and Technique* (3rd ed.). New York, NY: Routledge.

60 Ciornai, S. (2016) "Gestalt Art Therapy: A Path to Consciousness Expansion". In D.E. Gussak and M.L. Rosal (eds) *The Wiley Handbook of Art Therapy*. Chichester, UK: John Wiley & Sons.

61 Malchiodi, C.A. (2012) "Humanistic Approaches." In C.A. Malchiodi (ed.) *Handbook of Art Therapy* (2nd ed.). New York, NY: Guilford Press.

62 Ciornai, S. (2016) "Gestalt Art Therapy: A Path to Consciousness Expansion." In D.E. Gussak and M.L. Rosal (eds) *The Wiley Handbook of Art Therapy*. Chichester, UK: John Wiley & Sons.

63 Rhyne, J. (2016) "Gestalt Art Therapy." In J.A. Rubin (ed.) *Approaches to Art Therapy: Theory and Technique* (3rd ed.). New York, NY: Routledge, p.214.

64 Moon, B.L. (2004) *Art and Soul: Reflections on an Artistic Psychology*. Springfield, IL: Charles C. Thomas. NOTE: Inspired by the story of Carl, pp.37–42.

65 Corey, G. (2017) *Theory and Practice of Counseling and Psychotherapy* (10th ed.). Boston, MA: Cengage Learning.

66 Corey, G. (2017) *Theory and Practice of Counseling and Psychotherapy* (10th ed.). Boston, MA: Cengage Learning; Malchiodi, C.A. and Rozum, A.L. (2012) "Cognitive-Behavioral and Mind-Body Approaches." In C.A. Malchiodi (ed.) *Handbook of Art Therapy* (2nd ed.). New York, NY: Guilford Press.

67 Beck, A.T. (1963) "Thinking and depression: I. Idiosyncratic content and cognitive distortions." *Archives of General Psychiatry 9*, 4, 324–333.

68 Beck, A.T., Rush, A.J., Shaw, B.F., and Emery, G. (1979) *Cognitive Therapy of Depression*. New York, NY: Guilford Press.

69 Corey, G. (2017) *Theory and Practice of Counseling and Psychotherapy* (10th ed.). Boston, MA: Cengage Learning; Malchiodi, C.A. and Rozum, A.L. (2012) "Cognitive-Behavioral and Mind-Body Approaches." In C.A. Malchiodi (ed.) *Handbook of Art Therapy* (2nd ed.). New York, NY: Guilford Press; Rosal, M. (2016) "Cognitive-Behavioral Art Therapy." In J.A. Rubin (ed.) *Approaches to Art Therapy: Theory and Technique* (3rd ed.). New York, NY: Routledge.

70 Rosal, M. (2016) "Cognitive-Behavioral Art Therapy." In J.A. Rubin (ed.) *Approaches to Art Therapy: Theory and Technique* (3rd ed.). New York, NY: Routledge; Corey, G. (2017) *Theory and Practice of Counseling and Psychotherapy* (10th ed.). Boston, MA: Cengage Learning; Rosal, M.L. (2016) "Cognitive-Behavioral Art Therapy Revisited." In D.E. Gussak and M.L. Rosal (eds) *The Wiley Handbook of Art Therapy*. Chichester, UK: John Wiley & Sons.

71 Rosal, M. (2016) "Cognitive-Behavioral Art Therapy." In J.A. Rubin (ed.) *Approaches to Art Therapy: Theory and Technique* (3rd ed.). New York, NY: Routledge; Rosal, M.L. (2016) "Cognitive-Behavioral Art Therapy Revisited." In D.E. Gussak and M.L. Rosal (eds) *The Wiley Handbook of Art Therapy*. Chichester, UK: John Wiley & Sons; Malchiodi, C.A. and Rozum, A.L. (2012) "Cognitive-Behavioral and Mind-Body Approaches." In C.A. Malchiodi (ed.) *Handbook of Art Therapy* (2nd ed.). New York, NY: Guilford Press.

72 Rosal, M. (2016) "Cognitive-Behavioral Art Therapy." In J.A. Rubin (ed.) *Approaches to Art Therapy: Theory and Technique* (3rd ed.). New York, NY: Routledge. Case inspired by the story of Karen, pp.344–349.

73 Malchiodi, C.A. and Rozum, A.L. (2012) "Cognitive-Behavioral and Mind-Body Approaches." In C.A. Malchiodi (ed.) *Handbook of Art Therapy* (2nd ed.). New York, NY: Guilford Press; Rappaport, L. and Kalmanowitz, D. (2013) "Mindfulness, Psychotherapy, and the Arts Therapies." In L. Rappaport (ed.) *Mindfulness and the Arts Therapies: Theory and Practice*. London: Jessica Kingsley Publishers; Warren, S.S. (2006) "An exploration of the relevance of the concept of 'flow' in art therapy." *International Journal of Art Therapy: Inscape 11*, 2, 102–110; Peterson, C. (2013) "Mindfulness-Based Art Therapy: Applications for Healing with Cancer." In L. Rappaport (ed.) *Mindfulness and the Arts Therapies: Theory and Practice*. London: Jessica Kingsley Publishers.

74 Corey, G. (2017) *Theory and Practice of Counseling and Psychotherapy* (10th ed.). Boston, MA: Cengage Learning; Riley, S. and Malchiodi, C.A. (2012) "Solution-Focused and Narrative Approaches." In C.A. Malchiodi (ed.) *Handbook of Art Therapy* (2nd ed.). New York, NY: Guilford Press.

75 Riley, S. and Malchiodi, C.A. (2012) "Solution-Focused and Narrative Approaches." In C.A. Malchiodi (ed.) *Handbook of Art Therapy* (2nd ed.). New York, NY: Guilford Press; Gantt, L. and Greenstone, L. (2016) "Narrative Art Therapy in Trauma Treatment." In J.A. Rubin (ed.) *Approaches to Art Therapy: Theory and Technique* (3rd ed.). New York, NY: Routledge.

76 Gantt, L. and Greenstone, L. (2016) "Narrative Art Therapy in Trauma Treatment." In J.A. Rubin (ed.) *Approaches to Art Therapy: Theory and Technique* (3rd ed.). New York, NY: Routledge. Inspired by the story of Katie, pp.354–355, 362–368.

77 Corey, G. (2017) *Theory and Practice of Counseling and Psychotherapy* (10th ed.). Boston, MA: Cengage Learning; Riley, S. and Malchiodi, C.A. (2012) "Solution-Focused and Narrative Approaches." In C.A. Malchiodi (ed.) *Handbook of Art Therapy* (2nd ed.). New York, NY: Guilford Press.

78 Corey, G. (2017) *Theory and Practice of Counseling and Psychotherapy* (10th ed.). Boston, MA: Cengage Learning.

79 Riley, S. and Malchiodi, C.A. (2012) "Solution-Focused and Narrative Approaches." In C.A. Malchiodi (ed.) *Handbook of Art Therapy* (2nd ed.). New York, NY: Guilford Press.

80 Allen, P. (2016) "Art Making as Spiritual Path: The Open Studio Process as a Way to Practice Art Therapy." In J.A. Rubin (ed.) *Approaches to Art Therapy: Theory and Technique* (3rd ed.). New York, NY: Routledge.

81 Rappaport, L. (2016) "Focusing-Oriented Art Therapy." In J.A. Rubin (ed.) *Approaches to Art Therapy: Theory and Technique* (3rd ed.). New York, NY: Routledge.

82 Allen, P. (2016) "Art Making as Spiritual Path: The Open Studio Process as a Way to Practice Art Therapy." In J.A. Rubin (ed.) *Approaches to Art Therapy: Theory and Technique* (3rd ed.). New York, NY: Routledge; Franklin, M. (2016) "Contemplative Wisdom Traditions in Art Therapy: Incorporating Hindu-Yoga-Tantra and Buddhist Perspectives in Clinical and Studio Practice." In J.A. Rubin (ed.) *Approaches to Art Therapy: Theory and Technique* (3rd ed.). New York, NY: Routledge.

83 Rappaport, L. (2016) "Focusing-Oriented Art Therapy." In J.A. Rubin (ed.) *Approaches to Art Therapy: Theory and Technique* (3rd ed.). New York, NY: Routledge, p.288.

84 Corey, G. (2017) *Theory and Practice of Counseling and Psychotherapy* (10th ed.). Boston, MA: Cengage Learning.

85   Corey, G. (2017) *Theory and Practice of Counseling and Psychotherapy* (10th ed.). Boston, MA: Cengage Learning; Talwar, S. (2010) "An intersectional framework for race, class, gender, and sexuality in art therapy." *Art Therapy: Journal of the American Art Therapy Association 27*, 1, 11–17.

86   Corey, G. (2017) *Theory and Practice of Counseling and Psychotherapy* (10th ed.). Boston, MA: Cengage Learning.

87   Talwar, S. (2010) "An intersectional framework for race, class, gender, and sexuality in art therapy." *Art Therapy: Journal of the American Art Therapy Association 27*, 1, 11–17.

88   Corey, G. (2017) *Theory and Practice of Counseling and Psychotherapy* (10th ed.). Boston, MA: Cengage Learning.

89   Corey, G. (2017) *Theory and Practice of Counseling and Psychotherapy* (10th ed.). Boston, MA: Cengage Learning; Sobol, B. and Howie, P. (2016) "Family Art Therapy." In J.A. Rubin (ed.) *Approaches to Art Therapy: Theory and Technique* (3rd ed.). New York, NY: Routledge.

90   Horovitz, E.G. and Eksten, S.L. (2009) *The Art Therapists' Primer: A Clinical Guide to Writing Assessments, Diagnosis, and Treatment.* Springfield, IL: Charles C. Thomas; Corey, G. (2017) *Theory and Practice of Counseling and Psychotherapy* (10th ed.). Boston, MA: Cengage Learning.

91   Hoshino, J. (2016) "Getting the Picture: Family Art Therapy." In D.E. Gussak and M.L. Rosal (eds) *The Wiley Handbook of Art Therapy.* Chichester, UK: John Wiley & Sons.

92   Sobol, B. and Howie, P. (2016) "Family Art Therapy." In J.A. Rubin (ed.) *Approaches to Art Therapy: Theory and Technique* (3rd ed.). New York, NY: Routledge; Hoshino, J. (2016) "Getting the Picture: Family Art Therapy." In D.E. Gussak and M.L. Rosal (eds) *The Wiley Handbook of Art Therapy.* Chichester, UK: John Wiley & Sons.

93   Ricco, D.L. (2016) "A Treatment Model for Marital Art Therapy: Combining Gottman's Sound Relationship House Theory with Art Therapy Techniques." In D.E. Gussak and M.L. Rosal (eds) *The Wiley Handbook of Art Therapy.* Chichester, UK: John Wiley & Sons.

94   Waller, D. (1993) *Group Interactive Art Therapy.* Hove, England: Brunner-Routledge, pp.37–38.

95   Ibid., pp.38–39.

96   Personal communication, L. Schmanke and G. Wolf Bordonaro, June 29, 2020.

97   Waller, D. (1993) *Group Interactive Art Therapy.* Hove, England: Brunner-Routledge, pp.39–40.

98   Williams, K. and Tripp, T. (2016) "Group Art Therapy." In J.A. Rubin (ed.) *Approaches to Art Therapy: Theory and Technique* (3rd ed.). New York, NY: Routledge, pp.420–423.

99   Hanes, M.J. (1995) "Utilizing road drawings as a therapeutic metaphor in art therapy." *American Journal of Art Therapy 34*, 1, 19.

100 Williams, K. and Tripp, T. (2016) "Group Art Therapy." In J.A. Rubin (ed.) *Approaches to Art Therapy: Theory and Technique* (3rd ed.). New York, NY: Routledge; Rosal, M.L. (2016) "Rethinking and Reframing Group Art Therapy: An Amalgamation of British and US Models." In D.E. Gussak and M.L. Rosal (eds) *The Wiley Handbook of Art Therapy.* Chichester, UK: John Wiley & Sons; Waller, D. (1993) *Group Interactive Art Therapy.* Hove, UK: Brunner-Routledge.

101 Yalom, I.D. with Leszcz, M. (2005) *The Theory and Practice of Group Psychotherapy.* Cambridge, MA: Basic Books (original work published Yalom 1970).

102 Ibid.

103 Ibid.

104 Rosal, M.L. (2016) "Rethinking and Reframing Group Art Therapy: An Amalgamation of British and US Models." In D.E. Gussak and M.L. Rosal (eds) *The Wiley Handbook of Art Therapy.* Chichester, UK: John Wiley & Sons.

105 Schmanke, L. (2012) "Art Therapy Group Models" [Class handout]. Department of Counselor Education, Emporia State University, Emporia, KS.

106 Corey, G. (2017) *Theory and Practice of Counseling and Psychotherapy* (10th ed.). Boston, MA: Cengage Learning.

107 Ibid.

108 Wadeson, H. (2016) "An Eclectic Approach to Art Therapy." In J.A. Rubin (ed.) *Approaches to Art Therapy: Theory and Technique* (3rd ed.). New York, NY: Routledge.

109 Corey, G. (2017) *Theory and Practice of Counseling and Psychotherapy* (10th ed.). Boston, MA: Cengage Learning.

110 Rubin, J.A. (2016) "Conclusion." In J.A. Rubin (ed.) *Approaches To Art Therapy: Theory and Technique* (3rd ed.). New York, NY: Routledge.

Special Populations

1   Rubin, J.A. (2010) *Introduction To Art Therapy: Sources and Resources* (2nd ed.). New York, NY: Routledge.

2   Rubin, J.A. (2005) *Child Art Therapy* (25th Anniversary ed.). Hoboken, NJ: John Wiley & Sons; Councill, T. (2016) "Art Therapy with Children." In D.E. Gussak and M.L. Rosal (eds) *The Wiley Handbook of Art Therapy*. Chichester, UK: John Wiley & Sons.

3   Brooke, S.L. (1995) "Art therapy: An approach to working with sexual abuse survivors." *The Arts in Psychotherapy 22*, 5, 447–466; Backos, A.K. and Pagon, B.E. (1999) "Finding a voice: Art therapy with female adolescent sexual abuse survivors." *Art Therapy 16*, 3, 126–132; Pifalo, T. (2007) "Jogging the cogs: Trauma-focused art therapy and cognitive behavioral therapy with sexually abused children." *Art Therapy 24*, 4, 170–175; Pifalo, T. (2006) "Art therapy with sexually abused children and adolescents: Extended research study." *Art Therapy 23*, 4, 181–185; Pifalo, T. (2002) "Pulling out the thorns: Art therapy with sexually abused children and adolescents." *Art Therapy 19*, 1, 12–22.

4   Hanes, M.J. (1997) "In focus. Producing messy mixtures in art therapy: A case study of a sexually abused child." *American Journal of Art Therapy 35*, 3, 70–73. NOTE: Case inspired by the story of Felicia.

5   Alter-Muri, S.B. (2017) "Art education and art therapy strategies for autism spectrum disorder students." *Art Education 70*, 5, 20–25; Schweizer, C., Spreen, M., and Knorth, E.J. (2017) "Exploring what works in art therapy with children with autism: Tacit knowledge of art therapists." *Art Therapy: Journal of the American Art Therapy Association 34*, 4, 183–191.

6   Martin, N. (2009) "Art therapy and autism: Overview and recommendations." *Art Therapy: Journal of the American Art Therapy Association 26*, 4, 187–190; Gabriels, R.L. and Gaffey, L.J. (2012) "Art Therapy with Children on the Autism Spectrum." In C.A. Malchiodi (ed.) *Handbook of Art Therapy* (2nd ed.). New York, NY: Guilford Press; Richardson, J.F. (2016) "Art Therapy on the Autism Spectrum: Engaging the Mind, Brain, and Senses." In D.E. Gussak and M.L. Rosal (eds) *The Wiley Handbook of Art Therapy*. Chichester, UK: John Wiley & Sons.

7   Safran, D.S. (2012) "An Art Therapy Approach to Attention-Deficit/Hyperactivity Disorder." In C.A. Malchiodi (ed.) *Handbook of Art Therapy* (2nd ed.). New York, NY: Guilford Press.

8   Ibid., p.193.

9   Cobbett, S. (2016) "Reaching the hard to reach: Quantitative and qualitative evaluation of school-based arts therapies with young people with social, emotional and behavioural difficulties." *Emotional and Behavioural Difficulties 21*, 4, 403–415; Cross, M. (2011) *Children with Social, Emotional and Behavioural Difficulties and Communication Problems: There Is Always a Reason*. London: Jessica Kingsley Publishers.

10 O'Farrell, K. (2017) "Feedback feeds self-identity: Using art therapy to empower self-identity in adults living with a learning disability." *International Journal of Art Therapy: Inscape 22*, 2, 64–72; Hackett, S.S., Ashby, L., Parker, K., Goody, S., and Power, N. (2017) "UK art therapy practice-based guidelines for children and adults with learning disabilities." *International Journal of Art Therapy: Inscape 22*, 2, 84–94; Hallas, P. and Cleaves, L. (2017) "'It's not all fun': Introducing digital technology to meet the emotional and mental health needs of adults with learning disabilities." *International Journal of Art Therapy: Inscape 22*, 2, 73–83; Burns, S. and Waite, M. (2019) "Building resilience: A pilot study of an art therapy and mindfulness group in a community learning disability team." *International Journal of Art Therapy: Inscape 24*, 2, 88–96.

11 Furneaux-Blick, S. (2019) "Painting together: How joint activity reinforces the therapeutic relationship with a young person with learning disabilities." *International Journal of Art Therapy 24*, 4, 169–180. NOTE: Case inspired by the story of Anna.

12 Miller, M. (2012) "Art Therapy with Adolescents." In C.A. Malchiodi (ed.) *Handbook of Art Therapy* (2nd ed.). New York, NY: Guilford Press; Riley, S. (1999) *Contemporary Art Therapy with Adolescents*. London: Jessica Kingsley Publishers; Linesch, D. (2016) "Art Therapy with Adolescents." In D.E. Gussak and M.L. Rosal (eds) *The Wiley Handbook of Art Therapy*. Chichester, UK: John Wiley & Sons.

13 Pelton-Sweet, L.M. and Sherry, A. (2008) "Coming out through art: A review of art therapy with LGBT clients." *Art Therapy: Journal of the American Art Therapy Association 25*, 4, 170–176; Bettergarcia, J.N. and Israel, T. (2018) "Therapist reactions to transgender identity exploration: Effects on the therapeutic relationship in an analogue study." *Psychology of Sexual Orientation and Gender Diversity 5*, 4, 423–431.

14   Hinz, L.D. (2006) *Drawing from Within: Using Art to Treat Eating Disorders*. London: Jessica
       Kingsley Publishers; Hunter, M. (2016) "Art Therapy and Eating Disorders." In D.E. Gussak and M.L.
       Rosal (eds) *The Wiley Handbook of Art Therapy*. Chichester, UK: John Wiley & Sons.
15   Wilson, M. (2012) "Art Therapy in Addictions Treatment." In C.A. Malchiodi (ed.) *Handbook of Art
       Therapy* (2nd ed.). New York, NY: Guilford Press; Schmanke, L. (2017) *Art Therapy and Substance
       Abuse: Enabling Recovery from Alcohol and Other Drug Addiction*. London: Jessica Kingsley
       Publishers; Wise, S. (2009) "Extending a Hand: Open Studio Art Therapy in a Harm Reduction
       Center." In S. Brooke (ed.) *The Use of Creative Therapies with Chemical Dependency Issues*.
       Springfield, IL: Charles C. Thomas.
16   Zubala, A., MacIntyre, D.J., and Karkou, V. (2017) "Evaluation of a brief art psychotherapy group
       for adults suffering from mild to moderate depression: Pilot pre, post and follow-up study."
       International Journal of Art Therapy: Inscape 22, 3, 106–117; Blomdahl, C., Wijk, H., Guregård, S.
       and Rusner, M. (2018) "Meeting oneself in inner dialogue: A manual-based phenomenological art
       therapy as experienced by patients diagnosed with moderate to severe depression." *The Arts in
       Psychotherapy 59*, 17–24; Wise, S. (2016) "On Considering the Role of Art Therapy in Treating
       Depression." In D.E. Gussak and M.L. Rosal (eds) *The Wiley Handbook of Art Therapy*. Chichester,
       UK: John Wiley & Sons.
17   Councill, T. (2012) "Medical Art Therapy with Children." In C.A. Malchiodi (ed.) *Handbook of Art
       Therapy* (2nd ed.). New York, NY: Guilford Press; Anand, S.A. (2016) "Dimensions of Art Therapy in
       Medical Illness." In D.E. Gussak and M.L. Rosal (eds) *The Wiley Handbook of Art Therapy*.
       Chichester, UK: John Wiley & Sons; Malchiodi, C.A. (2012) "Using Art Therapy with Medical
       Support Groups." In C.A. Malchiodi (ed.) *Handbook of Art Therapy* (2nd ed.). New York, NY:
       Guilford Press.
18   Haeyen, S., van Hooren, S., Dehue, F., and Hutschemaekers, G. (2018) "Development of an
       art-therapy intervention for patients with personality disorders: An intervention mapping study."
       International Journal of Art Therapy: Inscape 23, 3, 125–135; Haeyen, S., van Hooren, S., and
       Hutschemaekers, G. (2015) "Perceived effects of art therapy in the treatment of personality
       disorders, cluster B/C: A qualitative study." *The Arts in Psychotherapy 45*, 1–10.
19   Eastwood, C. (2012) "Art therapy with women with borderline personality disorder: A feminist
       perspective." *International Journal of Art Therapy: Inscape 17*, 3, 98–114. NOTE: Case inspired by
       the story of Jo, pp.105–111.
20   Deegan, P. (1996) "Recovery as a journey of the heart." *Psychiatric Rehabilitation Journal 19*, 3,
       91–97; Spaniol, S. (2012) "Art Therapy with Adults with Severe Mental Illness." In C.A. Malchiodi
       (ed.) *Handbook of Art Therapy* (2nd ed.). New York, NY: Guilford Press; Patterson, S., Crawford, M.,
       Ainsworth, E., and Waller, D. (2011) "Art therapy for people diagnosed with schizophrenia:
       Therapists' views about what changes, how and for whom." *International Journal of Art Therapy:
       Inscape 16*, 2, 70–80.
21   Worden, W. (2002) *Grief Counseling and Grief Therapy* (3rd ed.). New York, NY: Springer; Rozum,
       A.L. (2012) "Art Therapy with Children in Grief and Loss Groups." In C.A. Malchiodi (ed.) *Handbook
       of Art Therapy* (2nd ed.). New York, NY: Guilford Press.
22   Malchiodi, C.A. (2007) *The Art Therapy Sourcebook*. New York, NY: McGraw-Hill; Kohut, M. (2011)
       "Making art from memories: Honoring deceased loved ones through a scrapbooking bereavement
       group." *Art Therapy: Journal of the American Art Therapy Association 28*, 3, 123–131.
23   Malchiodi, C.A. and Miller, G. (2012) "Art Therapy and Domestic Violence." In C.A. Malchiodi (ed.)
       Handbook of Art Therapy (2nd ed.). New York, NY: Guilford Press; Bird, J. (2018) "Art therapy,
       arts-based research and transitional stories of domestic violence and abuse." *International
       Journal of Art Therapy: Inscape 23*, 1, 14–24; Miller, G. (2009) "Bruce Perry's impact:
       Considerations for art therapy and children from violent homes." Retrieved from
       www.slideshare.net/gretchenmilleratrbc/PerryAATAPanelGretchen2; Walker, L.E. (2017) *The
       Battered Woman Syndrome* (4th ed.). New York, NY: Springer.
24   Prescott, M.V., Sekendur, B., Bailey, B., and Hoshino, J. (2008) "Art making as a component and
       facilitator of resiliency with homeless youth." *Art Therapy 25*, 4, 156–163; Griffith, F.J., Seymour, L.,
       and Goldberg, M. (2015) "Reframing art therapy to meet psychosocial and financial needs in
       homelessness." *The Arts in Psychotherapy 46*, 33–40; Feen-Calligan, H. (2016) "Art Therapy,
       Homelessness, and Poverty." In D.E. Gussak and M.L. Rosal (eds) *The Wiley Handbook of Art
       Therapy*. Chichester, UK: John Wiley & Sons.

25 Malchiodi, C.A. (2012) "Art Therapy with Combat Veterans and Military Personnel." In C.A. Malchiodi (ed.) *Handbook of Art Therapy* (2nd ed.). New York, NY: Guilford Press; Lobban, J. and Murphy, D. (2018) "Using art therapy to overcome avoidance in veterans with chronic post-traumatic stress disorder." *International Journal of Art Therapy 23*, 3, 99–114; Palmer, E., Hill, K., Lobban, J., and Murphy, D. (2017) "Veterans' perspectives on the acceptability of art therapy: A mixed-methods study." *International Journal of Art Therapy: Inscape 22*, 3, 132–137; Avrahami, D. (2006) "Visual art therapy's unique contribution in the treatment of post-traumatic stress disorders." *Journal of Trauma & Dissociation 6*, 4, 5–38; Kopytin, A. and Lebedev, A. (2013) "Humor, self-attitude, emotions, and cognitions in group art therapy with war veterans." *Art Therapy: Journal of the American Art Therapy Association 30*, 1, 20–29.
26 Lobban, J. and Murphy, D. (2018) "Using art therapy to overcome avoidance in veterans with chronic post-traumatic stress disorder." *International Journal of Art Therapy 23*, 3, 99–114. NOTE: Case inspired by the story of Mr. B, pp.100–112.
27 Rubin, J.A. (2010) "People We Serve." In J.A. Rubin, *Introduction to Art Therapy: Sources and Resources* (2nd ed.). New York, NY: Routledge; Yaretzky, A. and Levinson, M. (1996) "Clay as a therapeutic tool in group processing with the elderly." *American Journal of Art Therapy 34*, 3, 75–82; Pike, A. (2016) "Art Therapy with Older Adults: A Focus on Cognition and Expressivity." In D. Gussak and M.L. Rosal (eds) *The Wiley Handbook of Art Therapy*. Chichester, UK: John Wiley & Sons.
28 Guseva, E. (2019) "Art therapy in dementia care: Toward neurologically informed, evidence-based practice." *Art Therapy: Journal of the American Art Therapy Association 36*, 1, 46–49; Tucknott-Cohen, T. and Ehresman, C. (2016) "Art therapy for an individual with late stage dementia: A clinical case description." *Art Therapy: Journal of the American Art Therapy Association 33*, 1, 41–45; Lusebrink, V.B. (2004) "Art therapy and the brain: An attempt to understand the underlying process of art expression in therapy." *Art Therapy: Journal of the American Art Therapy Association 21*, 125–135.
29 Gonzalez-Dolginko, B. (2002) "In the shadows of terror: A community neighboring the World Trade Center disaster uses art therapy to process trauma." *Art Therapy 19*, 3, 120–122; Jones, J.G. (1999) "Mental health intervention in the aftermath of a mass casualty disaster." *Traumatology 5*, 3, 7–19; Chilcote, R.L. (2007) "Art therapy with child tsunami survivors in Sri Lanka." *Art Therapy 24*, 4, 156–162.
30 Chilcote, R.L. (2007) "Art therapy with child tsunami survivors in Sri Lanka." *Art Therapy 24*, 4, 156–162.
31 Ibid., p.159.
32 Czamanski-Cohen, J. (2010) "'Oh! Now I remember': The use of a studio approach to art therapy with internally displaced people." *The Arts in Psychotherapy 37*, 5, 407–413; Akthar, Z. and Lovell, A. (2019) "Art therapy with refugee children: A qualitative study explored through the lens of art therapists and their experiences." *International Journal of Art Therapy 24*, 3, 139–148.

Techniques and Directives

1 Rubin, J.A. (2010) *Introduction to Art Therapy: Sources and Resources* (2nd ed.). New York, NY: Routledge. NOTE: Information from p.155.
2 "Atom Conceptualization": personal communication, G. Wolf Bordonaro, April 12, 2019.
3 Malchiodi, C.A. (2007) *The Art Therapy Sourcebook*. New York, NY: McGraw-Hill.
4 Williams, K. and Tripp, T. (2016) "Group Art Therapy." In J.A. Rubin (ed.) *Approaches to Art Therapy: Theory and Technique* (3rd ed.). New York, NY: Routledge.
5 Buchalter, S.I. (2009) *Art Therapy Techniques and Applications*. London: Jessica Kingsley Publishers.
6 Liebmann, M. (2004) *Art Therapy for Groups: A Handbook of Themes and Exercises* (2nd ed.). Hove, UK: Routledge.
7 Junge, M.B. (2010) *The Modern History of Art Therapy in the United States*. Springfield, IL: Charles C. Thomas.
8 Malchiodi, C.A. (2012) "Psychoanalytic, Analytic, and Object Relations Approaches." In C.A. Malchiodi (ed.) *Handbook of Art Therapy* (2nd ed.). New York, NY: Guilford Press.

9   Winnicott, D.W. (1971) *Therapeutic Consultations in Child Psychiatry*. London: Hogarth.
10 Lusebrink, V.B. (1990) *Imagery and Visual Expression in Therapy*. New York, NY: Plenum Press.
11 Kramer, E. and Gerity, L.A. (2000) *Art as Therapy: Collected Papers*. London: Jessica Kingsley Publishers.
12 Mandali, M. (1991) *Everyone's Mandala Coloring Book*. Guilford, CT: Globe Pequot; Mehlomakulu, C. (2012, November 5) "Mandalas" [Blog post]. Creativity in Therapy. Retrieved from http://creativityintherapy.com/2012/11/mandalas
13 Malchiodi, C.A. (2007) *The Art Therapy Sourcebook*. New York, NY: McGraw-Hill.
14 Liebmann, M. (2004) *Art Therapy for Groups: A Handbook of Themes and Exercises* (2nd ed.). Hove, UK: Routledge.
15 Ibid., p.191.
16 Jones, J.G. (1999) "Mental health intervention in the aftermath of a mass casualty disaster." *Traumatology 5*, 3, 7–19.
17 Ibid., p.13.
18 Mehlomakulu, C. (2019, February 17) "Protective containers—Using art to strengthen the metaphor" [Blog post]. Creativity in Therapy. Retrieved from http://creativityintherapy.com /2019/02/protective-containers-using-art-strengthen-metaphor
19 Ibid.
20 Buchalter, S.I. (2009) *Art Therapy Techniques and Applications*. London: Jessica Kingsley Publishers, p.162.
21 Ibid., p.155.
22 Buchalter, S.I. (2004) *A Practical Art Therapy*. London: Jessica Kingsley Publishers.
23 Liebmann, M. (2004) *Art Therapy for Groups: A Handbook of Themes and Exercises* (2nd ed.). Hove, UK: Routledge.
24 Buchalter, S.I. (2004) *A Practical Art Therapy*. London: Jessica Kingsley Publishers.
25 Ibid., p.177.
26 Woolhiser Stallings, J. (2016) "Collage as an Expressive Medium in Art Therapy." In D.E. Gussak and M.L. Rosal (eds) *The Wiley Handbook of Art Therapy*. Chichester, UK: John Wiley & Sons.
27 Buchalter, S.I. (2009) *Art Therapy Techniques and Applications*. London: Jessica Kingsley Publishers, pp.108–115.
28 Wolf Bordonaro, G.P., Blake, A., Corrington, D., Fanders, T., and Morley, L. (2009) "Exploring media processes and project applications: (Re)discovering Shrinky Dinks®." *Arts and Activities 145*, 5, 28–29 and 64.
29 Schreiner, L. and Wolf Bordonaro, G.P. (2019) "Using nontraditional curricular tools to address death and dying in nurse education." *Journal of Hospice & Palliative Nursing 21*, 3, 229–236.
30 Orr, P. (2010) "Social Remixing: Art Therapy Media in the Digital Age." In C.H. Moon (ed.) *Materials and Media in Art Therapy: Critical Understandings of Diverse Artistic Vocabularies*. New York, NY: Routledge.
31 Orr, P. (2012) "Technology use in art therapy practice: 2004 and 2011 comparison." *The Arts in Psychotherapy 39*, 4, 234–238.
32 Thong, S.A. (2007) "Redefining the tools of art therapy." *Art Therapy 24*, 2, 52–58.
33 Kavitski, J. (2018) "The Animation Project." In C. Malchiodi (ed.) *The Handbook of Art Therapy and Digital Technology*. London: Jessica Kingsley Publishers.
34 Johnson, J.L. (2018) "Therapeutic Filmmaking." In C. Malchiodi (ed.) *The Handbook of Art Therapy and Digital Technology*. London: Jessica Kingsley Publishers.
35 Brown, C. and Garner, R. (2017) "Serious Gaming, Virtual, and Immersive Environments in Art Therapy." In R.L. Garner (ed.) *Digital Art Therapy: Material, Methods, and Applications*. London: Jessica Kingsley Publishers.
36 Jones, G., Rahman, R., and Robson, M. (2018) "Group Art Therapy and Telemedicine." In C. Malchiodi (ed.) *The Handbook of Art Therapy and Digital Technology*. London: Jessica Kingsley Publishers.
37 Wolf Bordonaro, G.P. (2014) "Tee-Shirt Art as an Expressive Therapeutic Intervention in Schools." In S. Degges-White and B.R. Colon (eds) *Expressive Arts Interventions for School Counselors*. New York, NY: Springer.
38 Malchiodi, C.A. (2007) *The Art Therapy Sourcebook*. New York, NY: McGraw-Hill.
39 Mims, R. (2016) "Using Visual Journaling to Promote Military Veteran Healing, Health and Wellness." In V. Buchanan (ed.) *Art Therapy: Programs, Uses, and Benefits*. Hauppauge, NY: Nova.
40 Jones, J.G. (1999) "Mental health intervention in the aftermath of a mass casualty disaster." *Traumatology 5*, 3, 7–19.

41   Liebmann, M. (2004) *Art Therapy for Groups: A Handbook of Themes and Exercises* (2nd ed.). Hove, UK: Routledge.
42   Drew, J. (2016) *Cartooning Teen Stories: Using Comics to Explore Key Life Issues with Young People*. London: Jessica Kingsley Publishers.
43   Fernandez, K.M. (2009) "Comic Addict: A Qualitative Study of the Benefits of Addressing Ambivalence through Comic/Cartoon Drawing with Clients in In-Patient Treatment for Chemical Dependency." In S.L. Brooke (ed.) *The Use of Creative Therapies with Chemical Dependency Issues*. Springfield, IL: Charles C. Thomas.
44   Buchalter, S.I. (2009) *Art Therapy Techniques and Applications*. London: Jessica Kingsley Publishers.
45   Liebmann, M. (2004) *Art Therapy for Groups: A Handbook of Themes and Exercises* (2nd ed.). Hove, UK: Routledge, p.222.
46   Malchiodi, C.A. (2007) *The Art Therapy Sourcebook*. New York, NY: McGraw-Hill.
47   Buchalter, S.I. (2009) *Art Therapy Techniques and Applications*. London: Jessica Kingsley Publishers.
48   Liebmann, M. (2004) *Art Therapy for Groups: A Handbook of Themes and Exercises* (2nd ed.). Hove, UK: Routledge.
49   Luzzatto, P., Sereno, V., and Capps, R. (2003) "A communication tool for cancer patients with pain: The art therapy technique of the body outline." *Palliative and Supportive Care 1*, 2, 135–142.
50   Hinz, L.D. (2006) *Drawing from Within: Using Art to Treat Eating Disorders*. London: Jessica Kingsley Publishers.
51   Martin, N. (2009) *Art as an Early Intervention Tool for Children with Autism*. London: Jessica Kingsley Publishers.
52   Hays, R.E. and Lyons, S.J. (1981) "The bridge drawing: A projective technique for assessment in art therapy." *The Arts in Psychotherapy 8*, 3–4, 207–217.
53   Ibid.
54   Holt, E. and Kaiser, D.H. (2009) "The First Step Series: Art therapy for early substance abuse treatment." *The Arts in Psychotherapy 36*, 4, 245–250, p.247.
55   Schmanke, L. (2017) *Art Therapy and Substance Abuse: Enabling Recovery from Alcohol and Other Drug Addiction*. London: Jessica Kingsley Publishers, p.103.
56   Ibid., pp.103–108.
57   Malchiodi, C.A. (2007) *The Art Therapy Sourcebook*. New York, NY: McGraw-Hill; Mehlomakulu, C. (2017, September 3) "Create a safe place" [Blog post]. Creativity in Therapy. Retrieved from http://creativityintherapy.com/2017/09/create-safe-place
58   Buchalter, S.I. (2009) *Art Therapy Techniques and Applications*. London: Jessica Kingsley Publishers.
59   Liebmann, M. (2004) *Art Therapy for Groups: A Handbook of Themes and Exercises* (2nd ed.). Hove, UK: Routledge.
60   Hanes, M.J. (1995) "Utilizing road drawings as a therapeutic metaphor in art therapy." *American Journal of Art Therapy 34*, 1, 19.
61   Liebmann, M. (2004) *Art Therapy for Groups: A Handbook of Themes and Exercises* (2nd ed.). Hove, UK: Routledge.
62   Hrenko, K.D. and Willis, R.W. (1996) "The amusement park technique in the treatment of dually diagnosed, psychiatric inpatients." *Art Therapy: Journal of the American Art Therapy Association 13*, 4, 261–264, p.261.
63   Ibid., p.262.
64   Moon, C.H. (2016) "Open Studio Approach to Art Therapy." In D.E. Gussak and M.L. Rosal (eds) *The Wiley Handbook of Art Therapy*. Chichester, UK: John Wiley & Sons.
65   Buchalter, S.I. (2009) *Art Therapy Techniques and Applications*. London: Jessica Kingsley Publishers, p.207.

Assessments

1   Schmanke, L. (2017) *Art Therapy and Substance Abuse: Enabling Recovery from Alcohol and Other Drug Addiction*. London: Jessica Kingsley Publishers.
2   Koppitz, E.M. (1968) *Psychological Evaluation of Children's Human Figure Drawings*. New York, NY: Grune & Stratton.

3   Brooke, S.L. (2004) *Tools of the Trade: A Therapist's Guide to Art Therapy Assessments* (2nd ed.). Springfield, IL: Charles C. Thomas.

4   Kaplan, F.F. (2012) "What Art Can and Cannot Tell Us." In C.A. Malchiodi (ed.) *Handbook of Art Therapy* (2nd ed.). New York, NY: Guilford Press.

5   Betts, D. (2016) "Art Therapy Assessments: An Overview." In D.E. Gussak and M.L. Rosal (eds) *The Wiley Handbook of Art Therapy*. Chichester, UK: John Wiley & Sons, pp.505–506.

6   Ulman, E. (1975) "A New Use of Art in Psychiatric Diagnosis." In E. Ulman and P. Dachinger (eds) *Art Therapy: In Theory and Practice*. New York, NY: Schocken.

7   Brooke, S.L. (2004) *Tools of the Trade: A Therapist's Guide to Art Therapy Assessments* (2nd ed.). Springfield, IL: Charles C. Thomas.

8   Ibid., p.58.

9   Ibid.

10   Cox, C.T., Agell, G., and Cohen, B.M. (2000) "Are you assessing what I am assessing? Let's take a look!" *American Journal of Art Therapy 39*, 2, 48–67.

11   Cohen, B.M. and Mills, A. (2016) "The Diagnostic Drawing Series (DDS) at Thirty: Art Therapy Assessment and Research." In D.E. Gussak and M.L. Rosal (eds) *The Wiley Handbook of Art Therapy*. Chichester, UK: John Wiley & Sons.

12   Rubin, J.A. (1973) "A diagnostic art interview." *Art Psychotherapy 1*, 1, 31–43.

13   Asawa, P. and Haber, M. (2016) "Family Art Assessment." In D.E. Gussak and M.L. Rosal (eds) *The Wiley Handbook of Art Therapy*. Chichester, UK: John Wiley & Sons.

14   Ibid.

15   Wadeson, H. (1980) *Art Psychotherapy*. New York, NY: John Wiley & Sons.

16   Burns, R.C. (1990) *A Guide to Family-Centered Circle Drawings*. New York, NY: Brunner/ Mazel.

17   Ibid., p.3.

18   Burns, R.C. and Kaufman, S.H. (1972) *Actions, Styles and Symbols in Kinetic Family Drawings* (K-F-D). New York, NY: Brunner/Mazel.

19   Brooke, S.L. (2004) *Tools of the Trade: A Therapist's Guide to Art Therapy Assessments* (2nd ed.). Springfield, IL: Charles C. Thomas.

20   Burns, R.C. and Kaufman, S.H. (1972) *Actions, Styles and Symbols in Kinetic Family Drawings* (K-F-D). New York, NY: Brunner/Mazel, p.5.

21   Brooke, S.L. (2004) *Tools of the Trade: A Therapist's Guide to Art Therapy Assessments* (2nd ed.). Springfield, IL: Charles C. Thomas; Burns, R.C. and Kaufman, S.H. (1972) *Actions, Styles and Symbols in Kinetic Family Drawings* (K-F-D). New York, NY: Brunner/Mazel.

22   Francis, D.M., Kaiser, D., and Deaver, S. (2003) "Representations of attachment security in Birds Nest Drawings of clients with substance abuse disorder." *Art Therapy Journal of AATA 20*, 3, 125–137; Kaiser, D. (1996) "Indicators of attachment security in a drawing task." *The Arts in Psychotherapy 23*, 4, 333–340.

23   Kaiser, D. (1996) "Indicators of attachment security in a drawing task." *The Arts in Psychotherapy 23*, 4, 333–340.

24   Brooke, S.L. (2004) *Tools of the Trade: A Therapist's Guide to Art Therapy Assessments* (2nd ed.). Springfield, IL: Charles C. Thomas.

25   Knoff, H.M. and Prout, H.T. (1985) "The Kinetic Drawing System: A review and integration of the kinetic family and school drawing techniques." *Psychology in the Schools 22*, 50–59.

26   Kramer, E. and Schehr, J. (2000) "An Art Therapy Evaluation Session for Children." In E. Kramer and L.A. Gerity (eds) *Art as Therapy: Collected Papers*. London: Jessica Kingsley Publishers.

27   Brooke, S.L. (2004) *Tools of the Trade: A Therapist's Guide to Art Therapy Assessments* (2nd ed.). Springfield, IL: Charles C. Thomas.

28   Buck, J.N. (1987) *The House-Tree-Person Technique: Revised Manual*. Los Angeles, CA: Western Psychological Services, p.18.

29   Brooke, S.L. (2004) *Tools of the Trade: A Therapist's Guide to Art Therapy Assessments* (2nd ed.). Springfield, IL: Charles C. Thomas.

30   Horovitz, E.G. and Eksten, S.L. (2009) *The Art Therapists' Primer: A Clinical Guide to Writing Assessments, Diagnosis, and Treatment*. Springfield, IL: Charles C. Thomas.

31   Koppitz, E.M. (1968) *Psychological Evaluation of Children's Human Figure Drawings*. New York, NY: Grune & Stratton.

32   Brooke, S.L. (2004) *Tools of the Trade: A Therapist's Guide to Art Therapy Assessments* (2nd ed.). Springfield, IL: Charles C. Thomas.

33   Koppitz, E.M. (1968) *Psychological Evaluation of Children's Human Figure Drawings*. New York, NY: Grune & Stratton, p.6.

34 Brooke, S.L. (2004) *Tools of the Trade: A Therapist's Guide to Art Therapy Assessments* (2nd ed.). Springfield, IL: Charles C. Thomas.
35 Gantt, L. and Tabone, C. (1998) *The Formal Elements Art Therapy Scale: The Rating Manual.* Morgantown, WV: Gargoyle Press.
36 Ibid.
37 Ibid.
38 Betts, D.J. (2003) "Developing a projective drawing test: Experiences with the Face Stimulus Assessment (FSA)." *Art Therapy: Journal of the American Art Therapy Association 20*, 2, 77–82.
39 Horovitz, E.G. and Eksten, S.L. (2009) *The Art Therapists' Primer: A Clinical Guide to Writing Assessments, Diagnosis, and Treatment.* Springfield, IL: Charles C. Thomas.
40 Betts, D.J. (2003) "Developing a projective drawing test: Experiences with the Face Stimulus Assessment (FSA)." *Art Therapy: Journal of the American Art Therapy Association 20*, 2, 77–82, p.81.
41 Mattson, D.C. and Betts, D. (2016) "The Face Stimulus Assessment (FSA)." In D.E. Gussak and M.L. Rosal (eds) *The Wiley Handbook of Art Therapy.* Chichester, UK: John Wiley & Sons.
42 Betts, D.J. (2013) *The Face Stimulus Assessment (FSA) Rating Manual* (2nd ed.). Washington, DC: Department of Art Therapy, George Washington University.
43 Horovitz, E.G. and Eksten, S.L. (2009) *The Art Therapists' Primer: A Clinical Guide to Writing Assessments, Diagnosis, and Treatment.* Springfield, IL: Charles C. Thomas; Brooke, S.L. (2004) *Tools of the Trade: A Therapist's Guide to Art Therapy Assessments* (2nd ed.). Springfield, IL: Charles C. Thomas; Earwood, C. and Fedorko, M. (2016) "Silver Drawing Test/The Draw-A-Story (SDT/DAS): Assessment Procedures." In D.E. Gussak and M.L. Rosal (eds) *The Wiley Handbook of Art Therapy.* Chichester, UK: John Wiley & Sons.
44 Brooke, S.L. (2004) *Tools of the Trade: A Therapist's Guide to Art Therapy Assessments* (2nd ed.). Springfield, IL: Charles C. Thomas.
45 Brooke, S.L. (2004) *Tools of the Trade: A Therapist's Guide to Art Therapy Assessments* (2nd ed.). Springfield, IL: Charles C. Thomas; Earwood, C. and Fedorko, M. (2016) "Silver Drawing Test/The Draw-A-Story (SDT/DAS): Assessment Procedures." In D.E. Gussak and M.L. Rosal (eds) *The Wiley Handbook of Art Therapy.* Chichester, UK: John Wiley & Sons.
46 Brooke, S.L. (2004) *Tools of the Trade: A Therapist's Guide to Art Therapy Assessments* (2nd ed.). Springfield, IL: Charles C. Thomas.
47 Horovitz, E.G. and Eksten, S.L. (2009) *The Art Therapists' Primer: A Clinical Guide to Writing Assessments, Diagnosis, and Treatment.* Springfield, IL: Charles C. Thomas. NOTE: The following source is cited as the original in Horovitz and Eksten's book: Horovitz-Darby, E.G. (1988) Art therapy assessment of a minimally language skilled deaf child. Proceedings from the 1988 University of California's Center on Deafness Conference: Mental Health Assessment of Deaf Clients: Special Conditions. Little Rock, AR: ADARA.
48 Horovitz, E.G. and Eksten, S.L. (2009) *The Art Therapists' Primer: A Clinical Guide to Writing Assessments, Diagnosis, and Treatment.* Springfield, IL: Charles C. Thomas.
49 Levick, M.F. and Siegel, C.A. (2016) "The Levick Emotional and Cognitive Art Therapy Assessment (LECATA)." In D.E. Gussak and M.L. Rosal (eds) *The Wiley Handbook of Art Therapy.* Chichester, UK: John Wiley & Sons.
50 Horovitz, E.G. and Eksten, S.L. (2009) *The Art Therapists' Primer: A Clinical Guide to Writing Assessments, Diagnosis, and Treatment.* Springfield, IL: Charles C. Thomas,
51 Pearson Assessments (2020) *Bender Visual-Motor Gestalt Test* | Second Edition. Retrieved from www.pearsonassessments.com/store/usassessments/en/Store/Professional-Assessments/Cognition-%26-Neuro/Bender-Visual-Motor-Gestalt-Test-%7CSecond-Edition/p/100000190.html?tab=product-details
52 Brannigan, G.G. and Decker, S.L. (2006) "The Bender-Gestalt II." *American Journal of Orthopsychiatry 76*, 1, 10–12.
53 Brannigan, G.G. and Decker, S.L. (2003) *Bender Gestalt II* (2nd ed.). Itasca, IL: Riverside.
54 Brooke, S.L. (2004) *Tools of the Trade: A Therapist's Guide to Art Therapy Assessments* (2nd ed.). Springfield, IL: Charles C. Thomas.
55 Landgarten, H.B. (1993) *Magazine Photo Collage.* New York, NY: Brunner/Mazel. As cited in Woolhiser Stallings, J. (2016) "Collage as an Expressive Medium in Art Therapy." In D.E. Gussak and M.L. Rosal (eds) *The Wiley Handbook of Art Therapy.* Chichester, UK: John Wiley & Sons, pp.9–11.
56 Ibid., p.9.

57 Brooke, S.L. (2004) *Tools of the Trade: A Therapist's Guide to Art Therapy Assessments* (2nd ed.). Springfield, IL: Charles C. Thomas.
58 Woolhiser Stallings, J. (2016) "Collage as an Expressive Medium in Art Therapy." In D.E. Gussak and M.L. Rosal (eds) *The Wiley Handbook of Art Therapy*. Chichester, UK: John Wiley & Sons.
59 Hammer, E.F. (1958) *The Clinical Application of Projective Drawings*. Springfield, IL: Charles C. Thomas. Cited in Willis, L.R., Joy, S.P. and Kaiser, D.H. (2010) "Draw-a-Person-in-the-Rain as an assessment of stress and coping resources." *The Arts in Psychotherapy 37*, 3, 233–239.
60 Verinis, J.S., Lichtenberg, E.F., and Henrich, L. (1974) "The Draw-A-Person in the rain technique: Its relationship to diagnostic category and other personality indicators." *Journal of Clinical Psychology 30*, 407–414.
61 Willis, L.R., Joy, S.P., and Kaiser, D.H. (2010) "Draw-a-Person-in-the-Rain as an assessment of stress and coping resources." *The Arts in Psychotherapy 37*, 3, 233–239, p.235.
62 Verinis, J.S., Lichtenberg, E.F., and Henrich, L. (1974) "The Draw-A-Person in the rain technique: Its relationship to diagnostic category and other personality indicators." *Journal of Clinical Psychology 30*, 407–414.
63 Horovitz, E.G. (2017) *Spiritual Art Therapy* (3rd ed.). Springfield, IL: Charles C. Thomas; Horovitz, E.G. and Eksten, S.L. (2009) *The Art Therapists' Primer: A Clinical Guide to Writing Assessments, Diagnosis, and Treatment*. Springfield, IL: Charles C. Thomas.
64 Horovitz, E.G. (2017) *Spiritual Art Therapy* (3rd ed.). Springfield, IL: Charles C. Thomas, pp.31–32.
65 Horovitz, E.G. and Eksten, S.L. (2009) *The Art Therapists' Primer: A Clinical Guide to Writing Assessments, Diagnosis, and Treatment*. Springfield, IL: Charles C. Thomas.
66 Ibid., p.14.
67 Kim, S. (2016) "Assessments and Computer Technology." In D.E. Gussak and M.L. Rosal (eds) *The Wiley Handbook of Art Therapy*. Chichester, UK: John Wiley & Sons.
68 Ibid., p.591.
69 Malchiodi, C.A. (2012) "A Brief Overview of Art-Based Assessments." In C.A. Malchiodi (ed.) *Handbook of Art Therapy* (2nd ed.). New York, NY: Guilford Press.
70 Cohen, B.M. and Mills, A. (2016) "The Diagnostic Drawing Series (DDS) at Thirty: Art Therapy Assessment and Research." In D.E. Gussak and M.L. Rosal (eds) *The Wiley Handbook of Art Therapy*. Chichester, UK: John Wiley & Sons.

Summary

1   Rubin, J.A. (2010) *Introduction to Art Therapy: Sources and Resources* (2nd ed.). New York, NY: Routledge.
2   Junge, M.B. and Newall, K. (2015) *Becoming an Art Therapist: Enabling Growth, Change, and Action for Emerging Students in the Field*. Springfield, IL: Charles C. Thomas, pp.118–153.
3   Talwar, S. (2016) "Creating Alternative Public Spaces: Community-Based Practice, Critical Consciousness, and Social Justice." In D.E. Gussak and M.L. Rosal (eds) *The Wiley Handbook of Art Therapy*. Chichester, UK: John Wiley & Sons.
4   Boston, C. (2016) "Art Therapy and Multiculturalism." In D.E. Gussak and M.L. Rosal (eds) *The Wiley Handbook of Art Therapy*. Chichester, UK: John Wiley & Sons; Corey, G. (2017) *Theory and Practice of Counseling and Psychotherapy* (10th ed.). Boston, MA: Cengage Learning.
5   Corey, G. (2017) *Theory and Practice of Counseling and Psychotherapy* (10th ed.). Boston, MA: Cengage Learning.
6   Talwar, S. (2016) "Creating Alternative Public Spaces: Community-Based Practice, Critical Consciousness, and Social Justice." In D.E. Gussak and M.L. Rosal (eds) *The Wiley Handbook of Art Therapy*. Chichester, UK: John Wiley & Sons.
7   Corey, G. (2017) *Theory and Practice of Counseling and Psychotherapy* (10th ed.). Boston, MA: Cengage Learning.
8   Talwar, S. (2016) "Creating Alternative Public Spaces: Community-Based Practice, Critical Consciousness, and Social Justice." In D.E. Gussak and M.L. Rosal (eds) *The Wiley Handbook of Art Therapy*. Chichester, UK: John Wiley & Sons, p.843.
9   Kaplan, F.F. (2016) "Social Action Art Therapy." In D.E. Gussak and M.L. Rosal (eds) *The Wiley Handbook of Art Therapy*. Chichester, UK: John Wiley & Sons, p.790.
10 Emporia State University (2004) "ESU art therapy program turns 30." *Teachers College Newsletter 12*, 4, p.2.

11 Junge, M.B. (2014) *Identity and Art Therapy: Personal and Professional Perspectives.* Springfield, IL: Charles C. Thomas, p.176.
12 Ibid., p.68.
13 Ibid., p.112.
14 Ibid., pp.99–100.
15 Ibid., p.178.
16 British Association of Art Therapists (2020) "Qualifying training courses for art therapists in the UK." Retrieved from www.baat.org/Assets/Docs/2020%20HCPC%20Validated%20Art%20Therapy%20MA%20Training.pdf
17 Commission on Accreditation of Allied Health Education Programs (2017) "Find a program." Retrieved from www.caahep.org/Accreditation/Find-a-Program.aspx
18 American Art Therapy Association (2017) "Selecting a master's program." Retrieved from https://arttherapy.org/art-therapy-selecting-education-program

References

Aach-Feldman, S. and Kunkle-Miller, C. (2016) "Developmental Art Therapy." In J.A. Rubin (ed.) *Approaches to Art Therapy: Theory and Technique* (3rd ed.). New York, NY: Routledge.

Akthar, Z. and Lovell, A. (2019) "Art therapy with refugee children: A qualitative study explored through the lens of art therapists and their experiences." *International Journal of Art Therapy 24*, 3, 139–148.

Allen, P. (2016) "Art Making as Spiritual Path: The Open Studio Process as a Way to Practice Art Therapy." In J.A. Rubin (ed.) *Approaches to Art Therapy: Theory and Technique* (3rd ed.). New York, NY: Routledge.

Alter-Muri, S.B. (2017) "Art education and art therapy strategies for autism spectrum disorder students." *Art Education 70*, 5, 20–25.

Amendt-Lyon, N. (2001) "Art and creativity in Gestalt therapy." *Gestalt Review 5*, 4, 225–248.

American Art Therapy Association (2017) "About art therapy." Retrieved from https://arttherapy-.org/about-art-therapy

American Art Therapy Association (2017) "Becoming an art therapist." Retrieved from https://artthera-py.org/becoming-art-therapist

American Art Therapy Association (2017) "Credentials and licensure." Retrieved from https://artthera-py.org/credentials-and-licensure

American Art Therapy Association (2017) "Definition of profession." Retrieved from www.arttherapy-.org/upload/2017_DefinitionofProfession.pdf

American Art Therapy Association (2017) "Educational standards." Retrieved from https://arttherapy-.org/educational-standards

American Art Therapy Association (2017) "Multicultural sub-committee." Retrieved from https://art-therapy.org/multicultural-sub-committee

American Art Therapy Association (2017) "Selecting a master's program." Retrieved from https://art-therapy.org/art-therapy-selecting-education-program

American Art Therapy Association (2017) "State advocacy." Retrieved from https://arttherapy-.org/state-advocacy

Anand, S.A. (2016) "Dimensions of Art Therapy in Medical Illness." In D.E. Gussak and M.L. Rosal (eds) *The Wiley Handbook of Art Therapy*. Chichester, UK: John Wiley & Sons.

Art Therapy Credentials Board, Inc. (2019) "About the credentials." Retrieved from www.atcb.org/New_Applicants/AboutTheCredentials

Asawa, P. and Haber, M. (2016) "Family Art Assessment." In D.E. Gussak and M.L. Rosal (eds) *The Wiley Handbook of Art Therapy*. Chichester, UK: John Wiley & Sons.

Avrahami, D. (2006) "Visual art therapy's unique contribution in the treatment of post-traumatic stress disorders." *Journal of Trauma & Dissociation 6*, 4, 5–38.

Backos, A.K. and Pagon, B.E. (1999) "Finding a voice: Art therapy with female adolescent sexual abuse survivors." *Art Therapy 16*, 3, 126–132.

Beck, A.T. (1963) "Thinking and depression: I. Idiosyncratic content and cognitive distortions." *Archives of General Psychiatry 9*, 4, 324–333.

Beck, A.T., Rush, A.J., Shaw, B.F., and Emery, G. (1979) *Cognitive Therapy of Depression*. New York, NY: Guilford Press.

Bettergarcia, J.N. and Israel, T. (2018) "Therapist reactions to transgender identity exploration: Effects on the therapeutic relationship in an analogue study." *Psychology of Sexual Orientation and Gender Diversity 5*, 4, 423–431.

Betts, D. (2016) "Art Therapy Assessments: An Overview." In D.E. Gussak and M.L. Rosal (eds) *The Wiley Handbook of Art Therapy*. Chichester, UK: John Wiley & Sons, pp.505–506.

Betts, D.J. (2003) "Developing a projective drawing test: Experiences with the Face Stimulus Assessment (FSA)." *Art Therapy: Journal of the American Art Therapy Association 20*, 2, 77–82.

Betts, D.J. (2013) *The Face Stimulus Assessment (FSA) Rating Manual* (2nd ed.). Washington, DC: Department of Art Therapy, George Washington University.

Bird, J. (2018) "Art therapy, arts-based research and transitional stories of domestic violence and abuse." *International Journal of Art Therapy: Inscape 23*, 1, 14–24.

Blomdahl, C., Wijk, H., Guregård, S. and Rusner, M. (2018) "Meeting oneself in inner dialogue: A manual-based phenomenological art therapy as experienced by patients diagnosed with moderate to severe depression." *The Arts in Psychotherapy 59*, 17–24.

Boston, C. (2016) "Art Therapy and Multiculturalism." In D.E. Gussak and M.L. Rosal (eds) *The Wiley Handbook of Art Therapy*. Chichester, UK: John Wiley & Sons.

Brannigan, G.G. and Decker, S.L. (2003) *Bender Gestalt II* (2nd ed.). Itasca, IL: Riverside.

Brannigan, G.G. and Decker, S.L. (2006) "The Bender-Gestalt II." *American Journal of Orthopsychiatry 76*, 1, 10–12.

British Association of Art Therapists (2016) "Art therapy information." Retrieved from www.baat.org/Assets/Docs/2018%20ART%20THERAPY%20TRAINING%20new%20details.pdf

British Association of Art Therapists (2020) "Qualifying training courses for art therapists in the UK." Retrieved from www.baat.org/Assets/Docs/2020%20HCPC%20Validated%20Art%20Therapy%20MA%20Training.pdf

British Association of Art Therapists (n.d.) "Career information." Retrieved from www.baat.org/Careers-Training/Career-Information

British Association of Art Therapists (n.d.) "What is art therapy?" Retrieved from www.baat.org/About-Art-Therapy

Brooke, S.L. (1995) "Art therapy: An approach to working with sexual abuse survivors." *The Arts in Psychotherapy 22*, 5, 447–466.

Brooke, S.L. (2004) *Tools of the Trade: A Therapist's Guide to Art Therapy Assessments* (2nd ed.). Springfield, IL: Charles C. Thomas.

Brown, C. and Garner, R. (2017) "Serious Gaming, Virtual, and Immersive Environments in Art Therapy." In R.L. Garner (ed.) *Digital Art Therapy: Material, Methods, and Applications*. London: Jessica Kingsley Publishers.

Buchalter, S.I. (2004) *A Practical Art Therapy*. London: Jessica Kingsley Publishers.

Buchalter, S.I. (2009) *Art Therapy Techniques and Applications*. London: Jessica Kingsley Publishers.

Buck, J.N. (1987) *The House-Tree-Person Technique: Revised Manual*. Los Angeles, CA: Western Psychological Services, p.18.

Burns, R.C. (1990) *A Guide to Family-Centered Circle Drawings*. New York, NY: Brunner/Mazel.

Burns, R.C. and Kaufman, S.H. (1972) *Actions, Styles and Symbols in Kinetic Family Drawings* (K-F-D). New York, NY: Brunner/Mazel.

Burns, S. and Waite, M. (2019) "Building resilience: A pilot study of an art therapy and mindfulness group in a community learning disability team." *International Journal of Art Therapy: Inscape 24*, 2, 88–96.

Chilcote, R.L. (2007) "Art therapy with child tsunami survivors in Sri Lanka." *Art Therapy 24*, 4, 156–162.

Ciornai, S. (2016) "Gestalt Art Therapy: A Path to Consciousness Expansion." In D.E. Gussak and M.L. Rosal (eds) *The Wiley Handbook of Art Therapy*. Chichester, UK: John Wiley & Sons.

Cobbett, S. (2016) "Reaching the hard to reach: Quantitative and qualitative evaluation of school-based arts therapies with young people with social, emotional and behavioural difficulties." *Emotional and Behavioural Difficulties 21*, 4, 403–415.

Cohen, B.M. and Mills, A. (2016) "The Diagnostic Drawing Series (DDS) at Thirty: Art Therapy Assessment and Research." In D.E. Gussak and M.L. Rosal (eds) *The Wiley Handbook of Art Therapy*. Chichester, UK: John Wiley & Sons.

Commission on Accreditation of Allied Health Education Programs (2017) "Find a program." Retrieved from www.caahep.org/Accreditation/Find-a-Program.aspx

Corey, G. (2017) *Theory and Practice of Counseling and Psychotherapy* (10th ed.). Boston, MA: Cengage Learning.

Councill, T. (2012) "Medical Art Therapy with Children." In C.A. Malchiodi (ed.) *Handbook of Art Therapy* (2nd ed.). New York, NY: Guilford Press.

Councill, T. (2016) "Art Therapy with Children." In D.E. Gussak and M.L. Rosal (eds) *The Wiley Handbook of Art Therapy*. Chichester, UK: John Wiley & Sons.

Cox, C.T., Agell, G., and Cohen, B.M. (2000) "Are you assessing what I am assessing? Let's take a look!" *American Journal of Art Therapy 39*, 2, 48–67.

Cross, M. (2011) *Children with Social, Emotional and Behavioural Difficulties and Communication Problems: There Is Always a Reason*. London: Jessica Kingsley Publishers.

Czamanski-Cohen, J. (2010) "'Oh! Now I remember': The use of a studio approach to art therapy with internally displaced people." *The Arts in Psychotherapy 37*, 5, 407–413.

Deegan, P. (1996) "Recovery as a journey of the heart." *Psychiatric Rehabilitation Journal 19*, 3, 91–97.

Drew, J. (2016) *Cartooning Teen Stories: Using Comics to Explore Key Life Issues with Young People.* London: Jessica Kingsley Publishers.

Earwood, C. and Fedorko, M. (2016) "Silver Drawing Test/The Draw-A-Story (SDT/DAS): Assessment Procedures." In D.E. Gussak and M.L. Rosal (eds) *The Wiley Handbook of Art Therapy.* Chichester, UK: John Wiley & Sons.

Eastwood, C. (2012) "Art therapy with women with borderline personality disorder: A feminist perspective." *International Journal of Art Therapy: Inscape 17*, 3, 98–114. NOTE: Case inspired by the story of Jo, pp.105–111.

Emporia State University (2004) "ESU art therapy program turns 30." *Teachers College Newsletter 12*, 4, p.2.

Feen-Calligan, H. (2016) "Art Therapy, Homelessness, and Poverty." In D.E. Gussak and M.L. Rosal (eds) *The Wiley Handbook of Art Therapy.* Chichester, UK: John Wiley & Sons.

Fernandez, K.M. (2009) "Comic Addict: A Qualitative Study of the Benefits of Addressing Ambivalence through Comic/Cartoon Drawing with Clients in In-Patient Treatment for Chemical Dependency." In S.L. Brooke (ed.) *The Use of Creative Therapies with Chemical Dependency Issues.* Springfield, IL: Charles C. Thomas.

Fish, B. (2013) "Reflections on the beginning of the ATCB." *ATCB Review 20*, 2, 1, 9. Retrieved from www.atcb.org/resource/pdf/Newsletter/Summer2013.pdf

Francis, D.M., Kaiser, D., and Deaver, S. (2003) "Representations of attachment security in Birds Nest Drawings of clients with substance abuse disorder." *Art Therapy Journal of AATA 20*, 3, 125–137.

Franklin, M. (2016) "Contemplative Wisdom Traditions in Art Therapy: Incorporating Hindu-Yoga-Tantra and Buddhist Perspectives in Clinical and Studio Practice." In J.A. Rubin (ed.) *Approaches to Art Therapy: Theory and Technique* (3rd ed.). New York, NY: Routledge.

Freud, S. (1989) "The ego and the id (1923)." *TACD Journal 17*, 1, 5–22.

Furneaux-Blick, S. (2019) "Painting together: How joint activity reinforces the therapeutic relationship with a young person with learning disabilities." *International Journal of Art Therapy 24*, 4, 169–180. NOTE: Case inspired by the story of Anna.

Gabriels, R.L. and Gaffey, L.J. (2012) "Art Therapy with Children on the Autism Spectrum." In C. Malchiodi (ed.) *Handbook of Art Therapy* (2nd ed.). New York, NY: Guilford Press.

Gantt, L. and Greenstone, L. (2016) "Narrative Art Therapy in Trauma Treatment." In J.A. Rubin (ed.) *Approaches to Art Therapy: Theory and Technique* (3rd ed.). New York, NY: Routledge.

Gantt, L. and Tabone, C. (1998) *The Formal Elements Art Therapy Scale: The Rating Manual.* Morgantown, WV: Gargoyle Press.

Garyfalakis, R. (2017) "What's the difference between art therapy and an art class?" Retrieved from www.artastherapy.ca/art-as-therapy-blog/2017/3/14/whats-the-difference-between-art-therapy-and-an-art-class

Gonzalez-Dolginko, B. (2002) "In the shadows of terror: A community neighboring the World Trade Center disaster uses art therapy to process trauma." *Art Therapy 19*, 3, 120–122.

Griffith, F.J., Seymour, L., and Goldberg, M. (2015) "Reframing art therapy to meet psychosocial and financial needs in homelessness." *The Arts in Psychotherapy 46*, 33–40.

Guseva, E. (2019) "Art therapy in dementia care: Toward neurologically informed, evidence-based practice." *Art Therapy: Journal of the American Art Therapy Association 36*, 1, 46–49.

Hackett, S.S., Ashby, L., Parker, K., Goody, S., and Power, N. (2017) "UK art therapy practice-based guidelines for children and adults with learning disabilities." *International Journal of Art Therapy: Inscape 22*, 2, 84–94.

Haeyen, S., van Hooren, S., and Hutschemaekers, G. (2015) "Perceived effects of art therapy in the treatment of personality disorders, cluster B/C: A qualitative study." *The Arts in Psychotherapy 45*, 1–10.

Haeyen, S., van Hooren, S., Dehue, F., and Hutschemaekers, G. (2018) "Development of an art-therapy intervention for patients with personality disorders: An intervention mapping study." *International Journal of Art Therapy: Inscape 23*, 3, 125–135.

Hallas, P. and Cleaves, L. (2017) "'It's not all fun': Introducing digital technology to meet the emotional and mental health needs of adults with learning disabilities." *International Journal of Art Therapy: Inscape 22*, 2, 73–83.

Hammer, E.F. (1958) *The Clinical Application of Projective Drawings.* Springfield, IL: Charles C. Thomas. Cited in Willis, L.R., Joy, S.P. and Kaiser, D.H. (2010) "Draw-a-Person-in-the-Rain as an assessment of stress and coping resources." *The Arts in Psychotherapy 37*, 3, 233–239.

Hanes, M.J. (1995) "Utilizing road drawings as a therapeutic metaphor in art therapy." *American Journal of Art Therapy 34*, 1, 19.

Hanes, M.J. (1997) "In focus. Producing messy mixtures in art therapy: A case study of a sexually abused child." *American Journal of Art Therapy 35*, 3, 70–73. NOTE: Case inspired by the story of Felicia.

Hays, R.E. and Lyons, S.J. (1981) "The bridge drawing: A projective technique for assessment in art therapy." *The Arts in Psychotherapy 8*, 3–4, 207–217.

Health & Care Professions Council (2019) "UK application forms." Retrieved from www.hpc-uk.org/registration/getting-on-the-register/uk-applications/uk-application-forms

Hinz, L.D. (2006) *Drawing from Within: Using Art to Treat Eating Disorders*. London: Jessica Kingsley Publishers.

Hinz, L.D. (2009) *Expressive Therapies Continuum: A Framework for Using Art in Therapy*. New York, NY: Routledge.

Holt, E. and Kaiser, D.H. (2009) "The First Step Series: Art therapy for early substance abuse treatment." *The Arts in Psychotherapy 36*, 4, 245–250, p.247.

Horovitz, E.G. (2017) *Spiritual Art Therapy* (3rd ed.). Springfield, IL: Charles C. Thomas.

Horovitz, E.G. and Eksten, S.L. (2009) *The Art Therapists' Primer: A Clinical Guide to Writing Assessments, Diagnosis, and Treatment*. Springfield, IL: Charles C. Thomas.

Hoshino, J. (2016) "Getting the Picture: Family Art Therapy." In D.E. Gussak and M.L. Rosal (eds) *The Wiley Handbook of Art Therapy*. Chichester, UK: John Wiley & Sons.

Hrenko, K.D. and Willis, R.W. (1996) "The amusement park technique in the treatment of dually diagnosed, psychiatric inpatients." *Art Therapy: Journal of the American Art Therapy Association 13*, 4, 261–264, p.261.

Hunter, M. (2016) "Art Therapy and Eating Disorders." In D.E. Gussak and M.L. Rosal (eds) *The Wiley Handbook of Art Therapy*. Chichester, UK: John Wiley & Sons.

Johnson, J.L. (2018) "Therapeutic Filmmaking." In C. Malchiodi (ed.) *The Handbook of Art Therapy and Digital Technology*. London: Jessica Kingsley Publishers.

Jones, G., Rahman, R., and Robson, M. (2018) "Group Art Therapy and Telemedicine." In C. Malchiodi (ed.) *The Handbook of Art Therapy and Digital Technology*. London: Jessica Kingsley Publishers.

Jones, J.G. (1999) "Mental health intervention in the aftermath of a mass casualty disaster." *Traumatology 5*, 3, 7–19.

Jung, C.G. (2014) *The Archetypes and the Collective Unconscious*. New York, NY: Routledge.

Junge, M.B. (2010) *The Modern History of Art Therapy in the United States*. Springfield, IL: Charles C. Thomas.

Junge, M.B. (2014) *Identity and Art Therapy: Personal and Professional Perspectives*. Springfield, IL: Charles C. Thomas.

Junge, M.B. and Newall, K. (2015) *Becoming an Art Therapist: Enabling Growth, Change, and Action for Emerging Students in the Field*. Springfield, IL: Charles C. Thomas.

Kagin, S.L. and Lusebrink, V.B. (1978) "The expressive therapies continuum." *Art Psychotherapy 5*, 171–180.

Kaiser, D. (1996) "Indicators of attachment security in a drawing task." *The Arts in Psychotherapy 23*, 4, 333–340.

Kaplan, F.F. (2012) "What Art Can and Cannot Tell Us." In C. Malchiodi (ed.) *Handbook of Art Therapy* (2nd ed.). New York, NY: Guilford Press.

Kaplan, F.F. (2016) "Social Action Art Therapy." In D.E. Gussak and M.L. Rosal (eds) *The Wiley Handbook of Art Therapy*. Chichester, UK: John Wiley & Sons, p.790.

Kavitski, J. (2018) "The Animation Project." In C. Malchiodi (ed.) *The Handbook of Art Therapy and Digital Technology*. London: Jessica Kingsley Publishers.

Kim, S. (2010) "A story of a healing relationship: The person-centered approach in expressive arts therapy." *Journal of Creativity in Mental Health 5*, 1, 93–98. 10.1080/15401381003627350. NOTE: Inspired by the story of Mrs. H.

Kim, S. (2016) "Assessments and Computer Technology." In D.E. Gussak and M.L. Rosal (eds) *The Wiley Handbook of Art Therapy*. Chichester, UK: John Wiley & Sons.

Knoff, H.M. and Prout, H.T. (1985) "The Kinetic Drawing System: A review and integration of the kinetic family and school drawing techniques." *Psychology in the Schools 22*, 50–59.

Kohut, M. (2011) "Making art from memories: Honoring deceased loved ones through a scrapbooking bereavement group." *Art Therapy: Journal of the American Art Therapy Association 28*, 3, 123–131.

Koppitz, E.M. (1968) *Psychological Evaluation of Children's Human Figure Drawings*. New York, NY: Grune & Stratton.

Kopytin, A. and Lebedev, A. (2013) "Humor, self-attitude, emotions, and cognitions in group art therapy with war veterans." *Art Therapy: Journal of the American Art Therapy Association 30*, 1, 20–29.

Kramer, E. and Gerity, L.A. (2000) *Art as Therapy: Collected Papers*. London: Jessica Kingsley Publishers.

Kramer, E. and Schehr, J. (2000) "An Art Therapy Evaluation Session for Children." In E. Kramer and L.A. Gerity (eds) *Art as Therapy: Collected Papers*. London: Jessica Kingsley Publishers.

Landgarten, H.B. (1987) *Family Art Psychotherapy: A Clinical Guide and Casebook*. New York, NY: Brunner/Mazel.

Landgarten, H.B. (1993) *Magazine Photo Collage*. New York, NY: Brunner/Mazel.

Levick, M.F. and Siegel, C.A. (2016) "The Levick Emotional and Cognitive Art Therapy Assessment (LECATA)." In D.E. Gussak and M.L. Rosal (eds) *The Wiley Handbook of Art Therapy*. Chichester, UK: John Wiley & Sons.

Liebmann, M. (2004) *Art Therapy for Groups: A Handbook of Themes and Exercises* (2nd ed.). Hove, UK: Routledge.

Linesch, D. (2016) "Art Therapy with Adolescents." In D.E. Gussak and M.L. Rosal (eds) *The Wiley Handbook of Art Therapy*. Chichester, UK: John Wiley & Sons.

Lobban, J. and Murphy, D. (2018) "Using art therapy to overcome avoidance in veterans with chronic post-traumatic stress disorder." *International Journal of Art Therapy 23*, 3, 99–114.

Lowenfeld, V. and Brittain, W.L. (1987) *Creative and Mental Growth* (8th ed.). Upper Saddle River, NJ: Prentice-Hall.

Lusebrink, V.B. (1990) "Levels of Expression and Systems Approach to Therapy." In V.B. Lusebrink (ed.) *Imagery and Visual Expression in Therapy*. Boston, MA: Springer.

Lusebrink, V.B. (1990) *Imagery and Visual Expression in Therapy*. New York, NY: Plenum Press.

Lusebrink, V.B. (2004) "Art therapy and the brain: An attempt to understand the underlying process of art expression in therapy." *Art Therapy: Journal of the American Art Therapy Association 21*, 125–135.

Luzzatto, P., Sereno, V., and Capps, R. (2003) "A communication tool for cancer patients with pain: The art therapy technique of the body outline." *Palliative and Supportive Care 1*, 2, 135–142.

Malchiodi, C.A. (2007) *The Art Therapy Sourcebook*. New York, NY: McGraw-Hill.

Malchiodi, C.A. (2012) "A Brief Overview of Art-Based Assessments." In C.A. Malchiodi (ed.) *Handbook of Art Therapy* (2nd ed.). New York, NY: Guilford Press.

Malchiodi, C.A. (2012) "Art therapy with Combat Veterans and Military Personnel." In C.A. Malchiodi (ed.) *Handbook of Art Therapy* (2nd ed.). New York, NY: Guilford Press.

Malchiodi, C.A. (2012) "Developmental Art Therapy." In C.A. Malchiodi (ed.) *Handbook of Art Therapy* (2nd ed.). New York, NY: Guilford Press.

Malchiodi, C.A. (2012) "Humanistic Approaches." In C.A. Malchiodi (ed.) *Handbook of Art Therapy* (2nd ed.). New York, NY: Guilford Press.

Malchiodi, C.A. (2012) "Psychoanalytic, Analytic, and Object Relations Approaches." In C.A. Malchiodi (ed.) *Handbook of Art Therapy* (2nd ed.). New York, NY: Guilford Press.

Malchiodi, C.A. (2012) "Using Art Therapy with Medical Support Groups." In C.A. Malchiodi (ed.) *Handbook of Art Therapy* (2nd ed.). New York, NY: Guilford Press.

Malchiodi, C.A. and Miller, G. (2012) "Art Therapy and Domestic Violence." In C.A. Malchiodi (ed.) *Handbook of Art Therapy* (2nd ed.). New York, NY: Guilford Press.

Malchiodi, C.A. and Rozum, A.L. (2012) "Cognitive-Behavioral and Mind-Body Approaches." In C.A. Malchiodi (ed.) *Handbook of Art Therapy* (2nd ed.). New York, NY: Guilford Press.

Mandali, M. (1991) *Everyone's Mandala Coloring Book*. Guilford, CT: Globe Pequot.

Martin, N. (2009) "Art therapy and autism: Overview and recommendations." *Art Therapy: Journal of the American Art Therapy Association 26*, 4, 187–190.

Martin, N. (2009) *Art as an Early Intervention Tool for Children with Autism*. London: Jessica Kingsley Publishers.

Maslow, A.H. (1943) "A theory of human motivation." *Psychological Review 50*, 4, 370–396.

Mattson, D.C. and Betts, D. (2016) "The Face Stimulus Assessment (FSA)." In D.E. Gussak and M.L. Rosal (eds) *The Wiley Handbook of Art Therapy*. Chichester, UK: John Wiley & Sons.

Mehlomakulu, C. (2012, November 5) "Mandalas" [Blog post]. Creativity in Therapy. Retrieved from http://creativityintherapy.com/2012/11/mandalas

Mehlomakulu, C. (2017, September 3) "Create a safe place" [Blog post]. Creativity in Therapy. Retrieved from http://creativityintherapy.com/2017/09/create-safe-place

Mehlomakulu, C. (2019, February 17) "Protective containers—Using art to strengthen the metaphor" [Blog post]. Creativity in Therapy. Retrieved from http://creativityintherapy.com/2019/02/protective-containers-using-art-strengthen-metaphor

Miller, G. (2009) "Bruce Perry's impact: Considerations for art therapy and children from violent homes." Retrieved from www.slideshare.net/gretchenmilleratrbc/PerryAATAPanelGretchen2.

Miller, M. (2012) "Art Therapy with Adolescents." In C.A. Malchiodi (ed.) *Handbook of Art Therapy* (2nd ed.). New York, NY: Guilford Press.

Mims, R. (2016) "Using Visual Journaling to Promote Military Veteran Healing, Health and Wellness." In V. Buchanan (ed.) *Art Therapy: Programs, Uses, and Benefits*. Hauppauge, NY: Nova.

Moon, B. (2016) "Art Therapy: Humanism in Action." In J.A. Rubin (ed.) *Approaches to Art Therapy: Theory and Technique* (3rd ed.). New York, NY: Routledge, p.204.

Moon, B.L. (2004) *Art and Soul: Reflections on an Artistic Psychology*. Springfield, IL: Charles C. Thomas.

Moon, B.L. (2009) *Existential Art Therapy: The Canvas Mirror* (3rd ed.). Springfield, IL: Charles C. Thomas.

Moon, C.H. (2010) *Materials and Media in Art Therapy: Critical Understandings of Diverse Artistic Vocabularies*. New York, NY: Routledge.

Moon, C.H. (2016) "Open Studio Approach to Art Therapy." In D.E. Gussak and M.L. Rosal (eds) *The Wiley Handbook of Art Therapy*. Chichester, UK: John Wiley & Sons.

Naumburg, M. (1966) *Dynamically Oriented Art Therapy: Its Principles and Practices*. New York, NY: Grune & Stratton.

O'Farrell, K. (2017) "Feedback feeds self-identity: Using art therapy to empower self-identity in adults living with a learning disability." *International Journal of Art Therapy: Inscape 22*, 2, 64–72.

Orr, P. (2010) "Social Remixing: Art Therapy Media in the Digital Age." In C.H. Moon (ed.) *Materials and Media in Art Therapy: Critical Understandings of Diverse Artistic Vocabularies*. New York, NY: Routledge.

Orr, P. (2012) "Technology use in art therapy practice: 2004 and 2011 comparison." *The Arts in Psychotherapy 39*, 4, 234–238.

Palmer, E., Hill, K., Lobban, J., and Murphy, D. (2017) "Veterans' perspectives on the acceptability of art therapy: A mixed-methods study." *International Journal of Art Therapy: Inscape 22*, 3, 132–137.

Patterson, S., Crawford, M., Ainsworth, E., and Waller, D. (2011) "Art therapy for people diagnosed with schizophrenia: Therapists' views about what changes, how and for whom." *International Journal of Art Therapy: Inscape 16*, 2, 70–80.

Pearson Assessments (2020) Bender Visual-Motor Gestalt Test | Second Edition. Retrieved from www.pearsonassessments.com/store/usassessments/en/Store/Professional-Assessments/Cognition-%26-Neuro/Bender-Visual-Motor-Gestalt-Test-%7CSecond-Edition/p/100000190.html?tab=product-details

Pelton-Sweet, L.M. and Sherry, A. (2008) "Coming out through art: A review of art therapy with LGBT clients." *Art Therapy: Journal of the American Art Therapy Association 25*, 4, 170–176.

Peterson, C. (2013) "Mindfulness-Based Art Therapy: Applications for Healing with Cancer." In L. Rappaport (ed.) *Mindfulness and the Arts Therapies: Theory and Practice*. London: Jessica Kingsley Publishers.

Pifalo, T. (2002) "Pulling out the thorns: Art therapy with sexually abused children and adolescents." *Art Therapy 19*, 1, 12–22.

Pifalo, T. (2006) "Art therapy with sexually abused children and adolescents: Extended research study." *Art Therapy 23*, 4, 181–185.

Pifalo, T. (2007) "Jogging the cogs: Trauma-focused art therapy and cognitive behavioral therapy with sexually abused children." *Art Therapy 24*, 4, 170–175.

Pike, A. (2016) "Art Therapy with Older Adults: A Focus on Cognition and Expressivity." In D. Gussak and M.L. Rosal (eds) *The Wiley Handbook of Art Therapy*. Chichester, UK: John Wiley & Sons.

Polster, E. and Polster, M. (1973) *Gestalt Therapy Integrated: Contours of Theory and Practice*. New York, NY: Brunner/Mazel.

Prescott, M.V., Sekendur, B., Bailey, B., and Hoshino, J. (2008) "Art making as a component and facilitator of resiliency with homeless youth." *Art Therapy 25*, 4, 156–163.

Rappaport, L. (2016) "Focusing-Oriented Art Therapy." In J.A. Rubin (ed.) *Approaches to Art Therapy: Theory and Technique* (3rd ed.). New York, NY: Routledge.

Rappaport, L. and Kalmanowitz, D. (2013) "Mindfulness, Psychotherapy, and the Arts Therapies." In L. Rappaport (ed.) *Mindfulness and the Arts Therapies: Theory and Practice*. London: Jessica Kingsley Publishers.

Rhyne, J. (2016) "Gestalt Art Therapy." In J.A. Rubin (ed.) *Approaches to Art Therapy: Theory and Technique* (3rd ed.). New York, NY: Routledge.

Ricco, D.L. (2016) "A Treatment Model for Marital Art Therapy: Combining Gottman's Sound Relationship House Theory with Art Therapy Techniques." In D.E. Gussak and M.L. Rosal (eds) *The Wiley Handbook of Art Therapy*. Chichester, UK: John Wiley & Sons.

Richardson, J.F. (2016) "Art Therapy on the Autism Spectrum: Engaging the Mind, Brain, and Senses." In D.E. Gussak and M.L. Rosal (eds) *The Wiley Handbook of Art Therapy*. Chichester, UK: John Wiley & Sons.

Riley, S. (1999) *Contemporary Art Therapy with Adolescents*. London: Jessica Kingsley Publishers.

Riley, S. and Malchiodi, C.A. (2012) "Solution-Focused and Narrative Approaches." In C.A. Malchiodi (ed.) *Handbook of Art Therapy* (2nd ed.). New York, NY: Guilford Press.

Robbins, A. (2016) "Object Relations and Art Therapy." In J.A. Rubin (ed.) *Approaches to Art Therapy: Theory and Technique* (3rd ed.). New York, NY: Routledge.

Rogers, C. (1951) *Client-Centered Therapy: Its Current Practice, Implications and Theory*. London: Constable.

Rogers, C.R. (1958) "A process conception of psychotherapy." *American Psychologist 13*, 4, 142–149.

Rogers, C.R. (1969) *Freedom to Learn: A View of What Education Might Become*. Columbus, OH: C.E. Merrill.

Rogers, N. (2016) "Person-Centered Expressive Arts Therapy: A Path to Wholeness." In J.A. Rubin (ed.) *Approaches to Art Therapy: Theory and Technique* (3rd ed.). New York, NY: Routledge.

Rosal, M. (2016) "Cognitive-Behavioral Art Therapy." In J.A. Rubin (ed.) *Approaches to Art Therapy: Theory and Technique* (3rd ed.). New York, NY: Routledge.

Rosal, M.L. (2016) "Cognitive-Behavioral Art Therapy Revisited." In D.E. Gussak and M.L. Rosal (eds) *The Wiley Handbook of Art Therapy*. Chichester, UK: John Wiley & Sons.

Rosal, M.L. (2016) "Rethinking and Reframing Group Art Therapy: An Amalgamation of British and US Models." In D.E. Gussak and M.L. Rosal (eds) *The Wiley Handbook of Art Therapy*. Chichester, UK: John Wiley & Sons.

Rozum, A.L. (2012) "Art Therapy with Children in Grief and Loss Groups." In C.A. Malchiodi (ed.) *Handbook of Art Therapy* (2nd ed.). New York, NY: Guilford Press.

Rubin, J. (2016) "Discovery and Insight in Art Therapy." In J.A. Rubin (ed.) *Approaches to Art Therapy: Theory and Technique* (3rd ed.). New York, NY: Routledge.

Rubin, J.A. (1973) "A diagnostic art interview." *Art Psychotherapy 1*, 1, 31–43.

Rubin, J.A. (2005) *Child Art Therapy* (25th Anniversary ed.). Hoboken, NJ: John Wiley & Sons.

Rubin, J.A. (2010) "People We Serve." In J.A. Rubin, *Introduction to Art Therapy: Sources and Resources* (2nd ed.). New York, NY: Routledge.

Rubin, J.A. (2010) *Introduction to Art Therapy: Sources and Resources* (2nd ed.). New York, NY: Routledge.

Rubin, J.A. (2011) *The Art of Art Therapy: What Every Art Therapist Needs to Know*. New York, NY: Routledge.

Rubin, J.A. (2016) "Conclusion." In J.A. Rubin (ed.) *Approaches To Art Therapy: Theory and Technique* (3rd ed.). New York, NY: Routledge.

Rubin, J.A. (2016) "Discovery and Insight in Art Therapy." In J.A. Rubin (ed.) *Approaches to Art Therapy: Theory and Technique* (3rd ed.). New York, NY: Routledge

Rubin, J.A. (2016) "Psychoanalytic Art Therapy." In D.E. Gussak and M.L. Rosal (eds) *The Wiley Handbook of Art Therapy*. Chichester, UK: John Wiley & Sons.

Rubin, J.A. (2016) *Approaches to Art Therapy: Theory and Technique* (3rd ed.). New York, NY: Routledge.

Safran, D.S. (2012) "An Art Therapy Approach to Attention-Deficit/Hyperactivity Disorder." In C.A. Malchiodi (ed.) *Handbook of Art Therapy* (2nd ed.). New York, NY: Guilford Press.

Schmanke, L. (2004) "Piaget's Stages of Cognitive Development" [Class handout]. Department of Counselor Education, Emporia State University, Emporia, KS.

Schmanke, L. (2005) "Erikson's Stages of Psychosocial Development" [Class handout]. Department of Counselor Education, Emporia State University, Emporia, KS.

Schmanke, L. (2012) "Art Therapy Group Models" [Class handout]. Department of Counselor Education, Emporia State University, Emporia, KS.

Schmanke, L. (2017) *Art Therapy and Substance Abuse: Enabling Recovery from Alcohol and Other Drug Addiction*. London: Jessica Kingsley Publishers.

Schmanke, L. (2018) "Developmental Art Therapy" [Class handout]. Department of Counselor Education, Emporia State University, Emporia, KS. Handout based on information from Rosal, M.L. (1996) *Approaches to Art Therapy for Children*. Burlingame, CA: Abbeygate.

Schmanke, L. (2018) "Freud" [Class handout]. Department of Counselor Education, Emporia State University, Emporia, KS.

Schmanke, L. (2018) "Mahler" [Class handout]. Department of Counselor Education, Emporia State University, Emporia, KS.

Schmanke, L. (2018) "Wrestling with Golomb—Summary Thoughts from Chapter 3" [Class handout]. Department of Counselor Education, Emporia State University, Emporia, KS.

Schreiner, L. and Wolf Bordonaro, G.P. (2019) "Using nontraditional curricular tools to address death and dying in nurse education." *Journal of Hospice & Palliative Nursing 21*, 3, 229–236.

Schweizer, C., Spreen, M., and Knorth, E.J. (2017) "Exploring what works in art therapy with children with autism: Tacit knowledge of art therapists." *Art Therapy: Journal of the American Art Therapy Association 34*, 4, 183–191.

Sobol, B. and Howie, P. (2016) "Family Art Therapy." In J.A. Rubin (ed.) *Approaches to Art Therapy: Theory and Technique* (3rd ed.). New York, NY: Routledge.

Spaniol, S. (2012) "Art Therapy with Adults with Severe Mental Illness." In C. Malchiodi (ed.) *Handbook of Art Therapy* (2nd ed.). New York, NY: Guilford Press.

Swan-Foster, N. (2016) "Jungian Art Therapy." In J.A. Rubin (ed.) *Approaches to Art Therapy: Theory and Technique* (3rd ed.). New York, NY: Routledge.

Talwar S. (2010) "An intersectional framework for race, class, gender, and sexuality in art therapy." *Art Therapy: Journal of the American Art Therapy Association 27*, 1, 11–17.

Talwar, S. (2016) "Creating Alternative Public Spaces: Community-Based Practice, Critical Consciousness, and Social Justice." In D.E. Gussak and M.L. Rosal (eds) *The Wiley Handbook of Art Therapy*. Chichester, UK: John Wiley & Sons.

Taylor & Francis Online (2020) *Canadian Art Therapy Association Journal*. Retrieved from www.tandfonline.com/toc/ucat20/current

Taylor & Francis Online (2020) *International Journal of Art Therapy*. Retrieved from www.tandfonline.com/loi/rart20

Thong, S.A. (2007) "Redefining the tools of art therapy." *Art Therapy 24*, 2, 52–58.

Tucknott-Cohen, T. and Ehresman, C. (2016) "Art therapy for an individual with late stage dementia: A clinical case description." *Art Therapy: Journal of the American Art Therapy Association 33*, 1, 41–45.

Ulman, E. (1975) "A New Use of Art in Psychiatric Diagnosis." In E. Ulman and P. Dachinger (eds) *Art Therapy: In Theory and Practice*. New York, NY: Schocken.

Verinis, J.S., Lichtenberg, E.F., and Henrich, L. (1974) "The Draw-A-Person in the rain technique: Its relationship to diagnostic category and other personality indicators." *Journal of Clinical Psychology 30*, 407–414.

Vick, R.M. (2012) "A Brief History of Art Therapy." In C.A. Malchiodi (ed.) *Handbook of Art Therapy* (2nd ed.). New York, NY: Guilford Press.

Wadeson, H. (1980) *Art Psychotherapy*. New York, NY: John Wiley & Sons.

Wadeson, H. (2016) "An Eclectic Approach to Art Therapy." In J.A. Rubin (ed.) *Approaches to Art Therapy: Theory and Technique* (3rd ed.). New York, NY: Routledge.

Walker, L.E. (2017) *The Battered Woman Syndrome* (4th ed.). New York, NY: Springer.

Waller, D. (1993) *Group Interactive Art Therapy*. Hove, UK: Brunner-Routledge.

Warren, S.S. (2006) "An exploration of the relevance of the concept of 'flow' in art therapy." *International Journal of Art Therapy: Inscape 11*, 2, 102–110.

Williams, K. and Tripp, T. (2016) "Group Art Therapy." In J.A. Rubin (ed.) *Approaches to Art Therapy: Theory and Technique* (3rd ed.). New York, NY: Routledge.

Willis, L.R., Joy, S.P., and Kaiser, D.H. (2010) "Draw-a-Person-in-the-Rain as an assessment of stress and coping resources." *The Arts in Psychotherapy 37*, 3, 233–239, p.235.

Wilson, M. (2012) "Art Therapy in Addictions Treatment." In C.A. Malchiodi (ed.) *Handbook of Art Therapy* (2nd ed.). New York, NY: Guilford Press.

Winnicott, D.W. (1971) *Therapeutic Consultations in Child Psychiatry*. London: Hogarth.

Wise, S. (2009) "Extending a Hand: Open Studio Art Therapy in a Harm Reduction Center." In S. Brooke (ed.) *The Use of Creative Therapies with Chemical Dependency Issues*. Springfield, IL: Charles C. Thomas.

Wise, S. (2016) "On Considering the Role of Art Therapy in Treating Depression." In D.E. Gussak and M.L. Rosal (eds) *The Wiley Handbook of Art Therapy*. Chichester, UK: John Wiley & Sons.

Wolf Bordonaro, G.P. (2014) "Tee-Shirt Art as an Expressive Therapeutic Intervention in Schools." In S. Degges-White and B.R. Colon (eds) *Expressive Arts Interventions for School Counselors*. New York, NY: Springer.

Wolf Bordonaro, G.P., Blake, A., Corrington, D., Fanders, T., and Morley, L. (2009) "Exploring media processes and project applications: (Re)discovering Shrinky Dinks®." *Arts and Activities 145*, 5, 28–29 and 64.

Woolhiser Stallings, J. (2016) "Collage as an Expressive Medium in Art Therapy." In D.E. Gussak and M.L. Rosal (eds) *The Wiley Handbook of Art Therapy*. Chichester, UK: John Wiley & Sons.

Worden, W. (2002) *Grief Counseling and Grief Therapy* (3rd ed.). New York, NY: Springer.

Yalom, I.D. with Leszcz, M. (2005) *The Theory and Practice of Group Psychotherapy*. Cambridge, MA: Basic Books (original work published Yalom 1970).

Yalom, I.D. (2002) *The Gift of Therapy: An Open Letter to a New Generation of Therapists and Their Patients*. New York, NY: HarperCollins.

Yaretzky, A. and Levinson, M. (1996) "Clay as a therapeutic tool in group processing with the elderly." *American Journal of Art Therapy 34*, 3, 75–82.

Zubala, A., MacIntyre, D.J., and Karkou, V. (2017) "Evaluation of a brief art psychotherapy group for adults suffering from mild to moderate depression: Pilot pre, post and follow-up study." *International Journal of Art Therapy: Inscape 22*, 3, 106–117.

Index